All books from Linkgua Ediciones feature Artificial Intelligence models trained by Hispanic studies experts. Ask your book's chat anything you wish about the work or its author.

For ebooks: Access our AI model through this link.

For printed books: Scan the QR code on the cover with your mobile device.

Get detailed analyses of our books, summaries, answers to your questions, and access our generative critical editions for a more enriching reading experience. Transparency and respect for the authorship of the sources used are fundamental to our project. Therefore, the responses offer, through a citation system, the sources with which they have been created.

Jorge Mañach y Robato

An Inquiry into Choteo

Translated and with an Introduction

by Jacqueline Loss

Barcelona 2024
Linkgua-ediciones.com

Credits

Original title: Indagación del choteo

© 2018, Red ediciones S.L.
© Jacqueline Loss

Translated by Jacqueline Loss
in collaboration with
Christina Bauman,
Morgan Handy,
Kevin Johnston,
Sonja Nishku,
and Jacqueline Slemp

e-mail: info@linkgua.com

Cover: Michel Mallard.
Cover image: 1917 Yearbook of the Cambridge High and Latin School

ISBN rústica ilustrada: 978-84-9897-354-9.
ISBN tapa dura: 978-84-1126-122-7.
ISBN ebook: 978-84-9953-950-8.

Contents

Acknowledgments

Without the help, support, and knowledge of various students, friends, and colleagues in different stages of translating *An Inquiry into Choteo*, this project would not have evolved into what it is. I greatly appreciate the willingness of my former undergraduates—Christina Bauman, Morgan Handy, Kevin Johnston, Sonja Nisku, and Jacqueline Slemp—to have accepted the somewhat irrational challenge of attempting to work as a group to translate this highly challenging essay. Ariana Hernandez-Reguant is partially responsible for that dare, and I thank her. After a semester, we achieved a very rough draft over which, for the past two and a half years, I have labored. Only, before the brilliant and meticulous comments and suggestions of Kristin Dysktra do I realize the full scope of this intellectual striptease. My consultations with Esther Allen from the start of the project similarly remind me how fortunate I am to be able to rely on such expertise. Yael Prizant also provided thought-provoking editorial work. My follies are my own. Lena Burgos-La Fuente, Enrique del Risco, Arturo López-Levy, Marilú Menéndez, María Pérez, Juan Carlos Quintero-Herencia, and Toba Leah Singer debated the meaning of the term *"parejería"* with me and helped me to carefully plot out its evolution in time and place. When my students and I had one of the most obscure questions, I approached the encyclopedic Víctor Fowler Calzada, who directed us to Ana Cairo Ballester; she solved our puzzle in no time. Odette Casamayor Cisneros, Ana Dopico, Rachel Price, Rafael Rojas, Vicky Unruh, Alexandra Vazquez, and Esther Whitfield all dedicated their precious time to reading my translation and/or introduction and led me to dig deeper into various topics. In addition, I would like to thank Susana Aho, María Antonia Cabrera

Arús, Rosa Helena Chinchilla, Julia Cuervo Hewitt, Matthew Corey, Augusto Espiritu, Isabel Garayta, Dara Goldman, Miguel Gomes, Andrew Hurley, Grettel Jiménez-Singer, Ellen Kanner Loss, Barbara Loss, Daniel Loss, Marilyn Miller, Amanda Moreno, Rolando Prats, Andrew N. Rubin, Sandra Ruiz, César Salgado, Miguel Sirgado, and Armando Suárez Cobián for helping me to sort out one detail or another, and in some cases, really, one detail after another. At a few key moments, I enormously appreciated the ability to rely on the first-rate translations of fragments of this essay, carried out by Gustavo Pérez Firmat. His previous scholarly reckoning with Mañach has helped me better understand this essay. A special thank you to Radamés Molina, a translator himself who has had *infinite* patience to dialogue with me continually down to the nitty-gritty of *criollo* phrases, and so much more.

Translator's Introduction

Positioning Choteo

Some years back, an esteemed professor whose seminar I adored brought me into his office to talk about my writing, from which he had gathered I was not a native English speaker. In fact, I am a native English speaker. But I felt obliged to imagine a justification for his query. I have inherited a less than perfect attachment to English idiomatic expressions and, in all likelihood, a few watered-down Germanic constructions that mutated into something else when they came into contact with my mostly elected affinities in Spanish. These characteristics can put me into an awkward position when it comes to translating, since, on occasion, I can be delayed to notice when foreign constructions are not entirely intelligible in English. However, more importantly, I appreciate the discomfort inspired by unusual constructions, taking grammar and style to be a mirror into individuals and the context in which they reside and express themselves. There is much to be said about the value of estrangement. Theorist Lawrence Venuti posed a challenge about fluency, bringing attention to "domestic values" that the translator inscribes within the texts through the decisions she makes. He goes so far as to say that: "A translator may find that the very concept of the domestic merits interrogation for its concealment of heterogeneity and hybridity which can complicate existing stereotypes, canons, and standards applied in translation."[1]

Even prior to translation, texts, in their original, are often wrestling with difference, with that belief in multiple communities of interpreters in a single nation; some of what in-

1   Lawrence Venuti, "Translation, Community, Utopia," *The Translation Studies Reader* (New York: Routledge, 2000), 469.

terests me in Jorge Mañach's *An Inquiry into Choteo* is the author's own discomfort. As a specialist in Cuban literature, I had prolonged coming to know this essay up close, on account of its cultural centrality and its rhetorical eccentricity. Only through a tedious and multi-step process of translation have I come to better understand why *An Inquiry into Choteo* is one of those essays which many Cubans would say, of course, that they have read, but that likely they have not in its entirety. And yet, the performance of "choteo," the performance of a certain attitude toward sobriety and jocularity, is far older than Mañach's original 1928 essay and continues to constitute an important aspect of Cubanía or Cubanness. The following explanation of Cuban "exceptionalism" provided by Louis A. Pérez, Jr. is important to keep in mind as we get to know Mañach's choteo.

> The forms through which Cubans developed the terms of collective self-awareness must themselves be understood as facets of the character of the Cuban: a people confident of a special destiny foretold in their history. At some point in the nineteenth century, Cubans developed the capacity to adopt an external vision as a perspective on themselves, to see themselves from the outside as a way to both contemplate the world at large and take measure of their place in that world. That they belonged they never doubted.[2]

Mañach's exploration of choteo is one of many such inquiries into the exceptionalism of the Cuban identity, a quest that has not disappeared in the present day.

As persistent as choteo remains in Cubans' collective memory are Cubans' ambivalent feelings toward it, not

2 Louis A. Pérez, Jr., *The Structure of Cuban History: Meanings and Purposes of the Past* (Chapel Hill: The University of North Carolina Press, 2013), 7.

just on the island, but in the diaspora as well. Attesting to choteo's longitude and malleability within global Cuban cultures is José Esteban Muñoz's invocation of it in his 1994 analysis of the queer Cuban-American feminist performers, Ela Troyano and Alina Troyano (whose stage name is Carmelita Tropicana). Muñoz suggests that for these sisters, choteo, like camp, is a strategy of cultural critique that "can be a style of colonial mimicry that is simultaneously a form of resemblance *and* menace." In so doing, Muñoz challenges what he sees as Mañach's "pathologizing" of choteo, viewing it instead as a "strategy of self-enactment that helps a colonized or otherwise dispossessed subject enact a self through a critique of the normative culture."[3]

The Vernacular Stranger

I would agree that Mañach pathologizes choteo, but there is much more. An unease is palpable throughout *An Inquiry into Choteo*, one, I would say, that corresponds not only to an emerging nation's necessity to gain "stable footing," but also to the author's individual experience as a postcolonial subject, who is, in turn, negotiating how, in the position of an intercontinental traveler, he also forms part of that emerging Cuban nation. In the 1920s, many of Cuba's intellectuals, like Mañach himself, were confronted with how to deal with a new postcolonial universe whose neocolonial leanings were undeniable. Following Cuba's independence from Spain, the United States significantly intervened in the Cuban economy, and, as Vicky Unruh maps, "Cuban intellectuals registered deep ambivalence toward the U.S. mar-

---

3   José Esteban Muñoz, *Disidentifications: Queers of Color and the Performance of Politics* (Minneapolis: University of Minnesota Press, 1994), 136.

ket-driven work ethic."[4] In turn, the performance of choteo, whose attitudinal traits include, mockery, levity, and distraction, puts a damper on the kind of sought-after, clear, transparent labor, associated with that work ethic.

As a translator and researcher, I have been compelled by the social and personal unease within Mañach's essay that nuances its frequently authoritative tone. Born in Sagua La Grande in Villa Clara, Cuba, in 1898, the final year of Cuba's war for independence, to a father from Galicia, of Catalan lineage, and a Cuban mother, Mañach began a life of travel at the age of nine, since his father opposed independence, and decided to move his family out of the new republic to live in Castilla-La Mancha, Spain. While that detail, in itself, does not entirely explain the participant/witness position that Mañach adopts toward the Cuban idiosyncrasy of choteo, it does shed light on some of his wavering within the essay: for instance, his shifting between the first-person singular (I) and plural (we) to the third-person singular (he, in this case) and plural (they), a device that is not uncommon within Cuban Spanish, but is somewhat more pronounced in Mañach, and his more explicit shift in positionality when he imagines what it could feel like to arrive in Cuba from abroad, almost like Alejo Carpentier in his 1939 well-known chronicle, "Havana seen by a Cuban Tourist." Mañach's rhetoric may sound somewhat antiquated to the 21st century reader whether in Spanish or in English. Its intricacies have been solidly studied by critics before me. For instance, José Prats Sariol deems Mañach's

4   Vicky Unruh, "Modernity's Labors in Latin America," in *The Oxford Handbook of Global Modernisms*, ed. Mark Wollaeger with Matt Eatough (New York: Oxford, 2012), 343.

style as reminiscent of 19th century modernism,[5] whereas Rafael Rojas suggests that it begins as impressionistic and moves toward more transparency. As Rojas delineates, this shift occurs in the process of Mañach's becoming more engaged with addressing the necessities of Cuban civil society.[6]

Mañach called himself the "forastero vernáculo"[7]— the "vernacular stranger" or the "vernacular foreigner"—terms that resonated as I tackled seemingly convoluted expressions. Mañach sets out to analyze choteo in an orderly fashion, yet choteo seems to continually escape the bounds of the territory that he claims it inhabits. That is to say that while sound bites of this essay abound, they fail to capture the entirety of the significance of the term for Mañach. In part, I would say that that insufficiency relates to Mañach's own "vernacularly strange" and inevitable performance.

In a slightly unpredictable manner that echoes Mañach, Gustavo Pérez Firmat gestures toward this challenge that Mañach's analysis of choteo presents to academic and cultural cooption. He describes how the author "carries the

---

5   José Prats Sariol, "Mañach y su fin de la cura," *Diario de Cuba*, January 9, 2018, http://www.diariodecuba.com/de-leer/1515533110_36491.html.

6   In *Motivos de Anteo: Patria y nación en la historia intelectual de Cuba* (Madrid: Colibrí, 2008), Rafael Rojas discusses what he sees as progress in Mañach's style: "In Mañach's work, it is possible to observe this stylistic progress from a fragmentary prose, expressed in the form of brief fictions or vignettes, like those in Glosario (1924) and *Estampas de San Cristóbal* (1926), toward a more sophisticated intellectual organization of the arguments, less prone to record 'impressions,' like those that appear in essays such as *La crisis de la alta cultura* (1925), *Indagación del choteo* (1928), *Historia y estilo* (1944) or *El espíritu de Martí* (1952)" (221). In my reading, *An Inquiry into Choteo* still bears traces of some of those earlier tendencies.

7   Duanel Díaz, *Mañach o la República* (Havana: Letras Cubanas, 2003), 72.

reader along without obstructing his path with detours of meaning or barriers to understanding" only to reveal that the essay is not "the straightforward, unencumbered exposition that it might at first appear to be," taking on the form of choteo, in its own "lapses of attention."[8] In so doing, he makes clear the centrality of "distraction" within Mañach's definition—a characteristic with which Cuban cinephiles are likely familiar. Mañach's preoccupation with Cubans' easy distraction may remind readers of the complaints of Sergio, the protagonist of Tomás Gutiérrez Alea's 1968 *Memories of Underdevelopment*, who, as he watches the Cuban people, and especially the women in his life, experience the revolution, utters: "One of the things that really gets me about people is their inability to sustain a feeling, an idea, without falling apart. Elena turned out to be totally inconsistent. It's pure alteration, as Ortega would say. She doesn't connect one thing with another. That's one of the signs of underdevelopment."[9]

Like Sergio, Mañach was an admirer of the Spanish philosopher, José Ortega y Gasset. His senior by only fifteen years, Ortega y Gasset was the focus of one of Mañach's most acclaimed essays, "Imagen de Ortega y Gasset," pub-

8   Gustavo Pérez Firmat, *Literature and Liminality: Festive Readings in the Hispanic Tradition* (Durham: Duke University Press, 1985), 53-54.

9   In Spanish, Sergio says, "Una de las cosas que más me desconcierta de la gente, es su incapacidad para sostener un sentimiento, una idea sin dispersión. Elena demostró ser totalmente inconsecuente. Es pura alteración, como diría Ortega. No le da relación a las cosas. Esa es una de las señales del subdesarrollo." The film's English subtitles translate Ortega y Gasset's concept of "*alteración*" (*Ensimismamiento y alteración*, 1939) as deterioration when, in fact, "alteration" would have been more philosophically precise. Alteration refers to the behavior of being taken by the world and living in an alienated manner.

lished one year after Mañach's 1955 revised edition of *An Inquiry into Choteo*.[10] Ortega y Gasset's influence resonates in Mañach's concern over the deformation of values and the disintegration of mass society. Like many others encountered in *An Inquiry into Choteo*, complaints over Cubans' inconsistency continue to be heard in the present. These days, however, rather than associate that trait with the transforming republic, Cubans attribute it to the failures of the revolution of 1959. As Mañach alternatively somberly critiques and values Cubans' tendency to not take anything seriously within *An Inquiry into Choteo*, readers may yearn for some comic relief, as they try to keep up with choteo's transforming meanings.[11]

But, beyond the transforming meanings, Mañach notes in the revised edition of his essay that the ubiquity of choteo has diminished over time, as a result of different experiences. In particular, in a footnote, he suggests that the revolutionary processes of the 1930s and 1940s led to tragic excesses that, in other words, diminished Cubans' propensity toward levity.

Mañach even remarks upon translation a couple of times within the essay (a fact that is not, at all, surprising, given that he, himself, translated, among others, George San-

10 *Indagación del choteo* (Lecture) was first published in *Revista de Avance* in Havana in 1928 and then La Verónica press in Havana published it in 1940. A 3rd revised edition was published by Editorial Libro Cubano in Havana in 1955. This translation is from *Indagación del choteo* (Barcelona: Linkgua ediciones, 2018).
11 I am grateful to Kristin Dykstra for her interview of me in *jacket2*, in which she encouraged me to begin commenting on this translation process.
    See Jacqueline Loss, "Out of synchness, taste, the slavic span, friends," by Kristin Dykstra, *jacket2*, August 21, 2015, http://jacket2.org/commentary/out-synchness-taste-slavic-span-friends.

tayana, around the time he was thinking about choteo).[12] First, translation becomes a topic when Mañach indicates the extent to which choteo translates into a form of mockery, and second, when he compares the early twentieth century comedies of the Spanish brothers Álvarez Quintero to Cuban choteo, revealing that their humor is likewise "difficult to translate." Pérez Firmat contrasts Mañach's negative view of Cuba's reliance on foreign models with his own positive perspective on Cuba's particular and original "translation sensibility."[13] For Narciso J. Hidalgo, this phrase overly emphasizes the easily assimilable elements of Cuban identity; that is, the intralingual translation on the Spanish-Cuban axis, rather than the African-Cuban one.[14] Other Cuban writers, including Fernando Ortiz, Mario Guiral Moreno, and José Antonio Ramos had already touched upon choteo when, in the 1925 *La crisis de la alta cultura* (The Crisis of High Culture), Mañach began to probe the concept, fueled by his desire to identify what Cuba misses in order for it to be civilized. Among the Europeans, the French were envisioned by Mañach as the most whole; and New Englanders were more charmed. The Spanish, more "civilized" than the "Poles" (as Cubans referred to Jews) and while the U.S. Americans may have brought Fords and so-called progress to the island, they were doing so in the absence of "civilization." In "The

12 See Rafael Rojas, "Dos Harvardians en la Habana," *Libros del crepúsculo*, December 21, 2013, http://www.librosdelcrepusculo. net/2013/12/dos-harvardians-en-la-habana.html.
13 Gustavo Pérez Firmat, *The Cuban Condition: Translations and Identity in Modern Cuban Literature* (New York: Cambridge University Press, 1989), 4.
14 Narciso J. Hidaglo, *Choteo. Irreverencia y humor en la cultura cubana* (Bogotá: Siglo del Hombre, 2012), 30.

Crisis of High Culture," Mañach critiques the Cuban culture of the first two decades of the Republic for its being plagued by a fear of standing out, and therefore, of being "choteado" or made a mockery of, so much so that "mockery ended up constituting the atmosphere, rarifying the moral air of the country."[15] That preoccupation with the nation's health pervades Mañach's two lectures, the first, delivered in 1925, before Fernando Ortiz, of the Sociedad Económica de Amigos del País, and the latter, in 1928, at the Institución Hispano-Cubana de Cultura, invited by Ortiz, and was already pervasive in other critics' assessments of choteo.

A distinguishing factor of Mañach's postulations is his insistence on the historical mechanism at work in choteo.[16] In contrast, Duanel Díaz notes that Ortiz and Mario Guiral Moreno understood choteo to be innate and that Guiral Moreno, in particular, critiqued José Miguel Gómez's government (1909-1913) for its leveling tendency that "hoisted up" blacks' position. The association of choteo with Afro-Cuban culture is also highlighted by Ortiz in *Los bailes y el teatro de los negros en el folklore de Cuba* (1951, Dance and Theater of Blacks in Folklore in Cuba), among other texts, where he suggests that choteo (mockery, inconsistency, spontaneity) extends from Afro-Cuban culture to the rest of Cuban society, having already lamented it as the "desgracia criolla" ("criollo misfor-

---

15 In the Spanish, "la mofa llegó a formar ambiente, enrareciendo el aire moral del país." Jorge Mañach, *La crisis de alta cultura en Cuba* (Barcelona: Linkgua Ediciones, 2011), 19.
16 Duanel Díaz, "Indagación de la chusmería," *Diario de Cuba*, September 14, 2013, http://www.diariodecuba.com/cultura/1379102842 _5058.html.

tune") many years before in a letter to the Spanish writer and philosopher, Miguel Unamuno.[17]

Mañach's choteo, in the words of Pérez Firmat, is "internal and external, congenital and learned, habitual and sporadic, malignant and benign"[18]—seeming contradictions that translation cannot fix. Instead, they become even more evident in English where they could be mistaken for errors or poor rendering of ideas. The beating around the bush and lack of succinct definition of "choteo" follows Mañach into English. For more succinct definitions, though, we could turn to Esteban Pichardo, who, in 1836, defines the adjective "choteado" as "ridiculous, defective, shoddy" and its verbal counterpart, as linked to the central region of the island, Villa Clara, where it means to mock, to make something ridiculous or defective."[19]

When I conveyed to a fellow translator my difficulty with Mañach's style, he simply uttered with a smile, "Well now you know what it's like for a Cuban in English, a language for which it seems everything has a solution." While this lucid explanation got to the heart of my frustrations in translating Cuban Spanish beyond this particular essay, I hesitated to entirely accept his quid pro quo analysis. Somehow it did not totally account for the peculiarity of the Mañach of *An Inquiry into Choteo*, a figure with whom, in Jorge Luis Arcos's reading, even Mañach's contemporaries took issue, in part, for his projecting an "uncomfortable distance, a sensation that he transmitted

17 Fernando Ortiz, *Entre Cubanos... (Psicología Tropical)* (Paris, Librería Paul Ollendorff, 1913), 7.

18 Pérez Firmat, *Literature and Liminality*, 55.

19 Esteban Pichardo, *Diccionario provincial casi razonado de vozes y frases cubanas* (1836) (Havana: Editorial de Ciencias Sociales, 1976), 218.

to whatever topic that he elaborated."[20] For instance, Unruh characterizes a discussion between Mariblanca Sabas Alomá (a Cuban feminist, journalist, and like Mañach, a co-founder of the Minorista group) and Mañach in the following fascinating manner:

> To [Mañach's] admonition that no writer was important enough to talk about themselves, she defended self-portraiture as a calculated strategy for connecting with readers, as a good teacher would do with students...intimating that the distance and complex language cultivated by Mañach itself constituted a strategic literary persona.[21]

Mañach's peculiarities might be better understood through more familiarity with his biography.

Mediation: the Subject and his Nation

The son of a loyalist, a position that was hardly unique at that time, Mañach was raised in Spain from the age of nine to fifteen. Reluctance to embrace independence affected even those without "Spanish blood," as David Sartorius explains. "Neither economic opportunity nor Spanish descent fully explains popular support for a colonial government that survived mainland Spanish American independence by many decades."[22] In 1913, Mañach returned to Cuba for two years, and soon thereafter, trav-

20 Jorge Luis Arcos, "Pensamiento y estilo en Jorge Mañach," *Temas* 16-17 (1998): 207.
21 Vicky Unruh, *Performing Women and Modern Literary Culture in Latin America: Intervening Acts* (Austin: University of Texas Press, 2016), 151.
22 David Sartorius, *Ever Faithful: Race, Loyalty, and the Ends of Empire in Spanish Cuba* (Durham: Duke University Press, 2013), xi.

eled to the United States, where he attended high school in Cambridge, Massachusetts and went on to receive a B.S. from Harvard in 1920. About his high school years, Mañach once revealed something that also sheds light on his evolving relationship to language: "I think that the first journalistic essay I published was in English, around 1916, in a little magazine that I co-edited at high school in Cambridge. I used to write in English, but I thought and felt in Spanish."[23] His success there helped him earn a scholarship to the Sorbonne, where he obtained a doctorate in Civil Law at a time when the international avant-garde was in full swing in Paris. Mañach could not help but partake and continued to once he returned to Cuba. In 1928, the same year he delivered *An Inquiry into Choteo*, he completed another doctorate in Philosophy and Letters at the University of Havana. Mañach also began regularly publishing vignettes in Cuban periodicals, such as *Diario de la Marina*, wherein, as Duanel Díaz notes, the young intellectual frequently negotiated his relationship to traditionalism and "progress," with Spain and the United States occupying opposing poles in this dichotomy. This background is crucial for us to keep in mind as we read *An Inquiry into Choteo* where, despite the United States not being named as a central culprit for Cubans' habitual refusal to take anything seriously in the Republic's early years, its disconcerting influence can be felt.

Mañach also became an active member of the Minorista group that "was made up of a nucleus of the aesthetic avant-

23 Rosario Rexach, *Dos figuras cubanas y una sola actitud: Félix Varela y Jorge Mañach* (Miami: Universal, 1991), 151. Thank you to Augusto Espiritu to calling my attention to this interesting detail.

garde, most of them against the republican status quo."[24] His fight against the regime of Alfredo Zayas (1921-1925) and then Gerardo Machado (1925-1933) led him to form part of the problematic ABC political organization against Machado, attacking the president's policies from the political right and even authoring, along with Joaquín Martínez Saenz, Francisco Ichaso, and Juan Andrés Lliteras, its manifesto. While the ABC claimed responsibility for terrorist attacks, from which Mañach later distanced himself, it is difficult to read the manifesto without hearing echoes of *An Inquiry into Choteo*. For instance, the manifesto's critique of the government's use of the lottery makes us recall Mañach's irritation with Cubans' predilection for gambling, already called a "devouring cancer," about a century before[25]; the manifesto's rabble-rousing discourse on a growing Antillean, black cheap labor and its effect on whites whose economic power, it says, is increasingly in the hands of "Wall Street," casts a different tone on Mañach's somewhat buried discussion of race in his 1928 essay. And when the manifesto yearns for the culture produced when Cuba was a colony of Spain, stating that Cuba's "subaltern culture" corresponds to the Republic's "parasitic economy," one cannot help but to similarly think back to Mañach's loyalist father and the postcolonial culture his son put under the microscope in *An Inquiry into Choteo*.

24 Ricardo Quiza Moreno, "New Knowledge for New Times: The Sociedad del Folklore Cubano during the 'Critical Decade'" in *State of Ambiguity: Civic Life and Culture in Cuba's First Republic*, edited by Stephen Palmer, José Antonio Piqueras, and Amparo Sánchez Cobos (Durham: Duke, 2014), 287, endote 20.

25 José Antonio Saco, *Memoria sobre la vagancia en Cuba* (Barcelona: Linkgua Ediciones, 2012), 13. This study was originally published in 1831 in the *Revista bimestre cubana*.

In that vein, José Duarte Oropesa, with Rafael Rojas following suit, emphasize the reliance in ABC's program upon ideas that emerged in earlier essays by Mañach, such as *An Inquiry into Choteo*, among others, and in particular, with regard to ABC's proposal for a radical nationalism capable of confronting the "U.S. political and economic encroachment" and its push for an "ethical rebirth, in the realms of education and culture."[26] The manifesto is firmly against Cubans' surrendering themselves (whether to the United States, their bosses, or the dictator).

In 1932, Mañach also founded the popular radio show La Universidad del Aire (the University on the Air), with the intent of disseminating culture to the people, a project he returned to years later. With such gestures toward Cuban sovereignty in mind, it might come as a surprise that when President Roosevelt sent Ambassador Welles in 1933 to undertake a "mediation," the ABC accepted the conditions and, for a brief time, became part of the new government. For a few months, Mañach was the "secretary for public instruction and fine arts," and, in that role, on page 2 of *The Brooklyn Daily Eagle* on May 28, 1934, appears his response to the attempted assassination of Ambassador Caffrey in Havana: "The Caffrey incident proves the necessity of the abolition of the Platt Amendment, as it would not have happened if a threat of United States intervention did not exist, in view of the fact that both Communists and Machadistas would like to see Cuba lose her sovereignty." When he left that post, he began editing the official newspaper of the ABC party, *Acción*. Facing more political problems with the closure of the newspaper, Mañach went into exile in the United States, and in 1935, he began teaching at

26 Rojas, *Motivos de Anteo*, 229.

Columbia University, as chair of Hispanic Studies, where he worked for a few years. If we consider Mañach's attitudes toward mediation and sovereignty, we can begin to sense the depths of these complex times. This Harvard-educated intellectual, author of an extreme manifesto, often deemed fascist, knew the United States up-close, and this knowledge is important to keep in mind while we read his pressing necessity to reveal Cuban traits in *An Inquiry into Choteo*.

As somewhat of an aside, despite my not wishing this introduction to serve as an exhaustive biography or critique of Mañach's work,[27] I cannot help but mention another episode in Mañach's family life that illustrates the proximity of Cuba and the United States. For, in 1937, his younger sister, Nena, wed Andrew Goodman, the owner of New York's famous department store Bergdorf Goodman, whom she had met on his vacation to Cuba.[28] I offer this tidbit to cast a slightly different tone upon Mañach in New York City, who had just helped to author a scathing manifesto, fiercely critical of interventions of the United States and Cuba's imitation of its constitution, and then, as brother-in-law to one of the Big Apple's most important businessmen.

By 1939, however, Mañach returned to Cuba, where he taught at the University of Havana, chairing an inaugural History of Philosophy. Ana Cairo evokes the image Mañach projected in those years by recalling a passage in Cintio

27 By the mid 1920's, Jorge was wed to Margot Baños, and they had one son.
28 The role of this Cuban matriarch, known as Dita, within the department store empire is even the subject of a 2001 documentary entitled *Dita and the Family Business*, directed by her grandson Joshua Taylor and Ferne Pearlstein.

Vitier's "fictionalized memory," the novel, *De Peña Pobre* (1979):

> The new professor seemed to be trying everything out for the first time; the recent chair earned fair and square. The repertory of explanations of being, the tight diction streaked with Catalan and Saxon inflections, the drill suit adjusted to his agile torso, the sparkling glasses over his aquiline nose..., his skeptic lips under his mustache, as groomed as his serious tie, fastened to his impeccable shirt. The guy looked like a stylish Unamuno, still young and without faith.[29]

In 1944, Mañach was even named foreign minister by Batista, a post which he renounced after a few months. By 1949, Mañach was back on the radio, reviving his popular show and launching, one year later, the television program, *Ante la Prensa* (Before the Press). After the U.S.-backed controversial dictator, Fulgencio Batista, seized the government in a 1952 coup d'etat, the University on the Air became a space where young intellectuals voiced their diverse and dissenting opinions. The radio show was even assaulted by Batista supporters. In the aftermath, Mañach left for Spain, coming in and out of Cuba until Batista was defeated. Ex-

29 "El Nuevo profesor parecía estar estrenándolo todo: la cátedra recién ganada en buena lid. El repertorio de explicaciones del ser, la dicción apretada, veteada de inflexiones catalanas y sajonas, el traje de dril ajustado al torso ágil, los espejuelos destellantes sobre la nariz aquilina, ... los labios escépticos bajo el bigote tan cuidado como la corbata sobria, sujeta por un pasador prendido a las puntas de la camisa impecable. Al muchacho le pareció un Unamuno atildado, todavía joven, y sin fe." Ana Cairo, "La polémica Mañach-Lezama-Vitier-Ortega," *Revista de la Biblioteca Nacional José Martí* (Enero-Junio 2002): 94.

tremely critical of communism, Mañach was equally critical of the corruption that plagued Batista's regime.

Also, between the mid-1940s and early 1950s, Mañach made extensive philosophical contributions, continuing to reflect upon the "possibilities of communication between the Hispanic and Anglo-Saxon intellectual traditions," something that he had already begun to do decades before. Furthermore, between 1947 and 1951, and then again, in 1955, Mañach spent six summers teaching Spanish courses at Middlebury College in Vermont.[30] In the process of Mañach's recuperation "within" the revolutionary discourse, especially by the likes of Ana Cairo,[31] Marta Rojas,[32] Rigoberto Segreo, and Margarita Segura,[33] came the revelation that Mañach wrote the prologue to a clandestine version of Fidel Castro's famous speech "History Will Absolve Me" that he delivered in court after the attack on Moncada in 1953.[34] In 1955, he became the first vice-president of the Cuban Association of the Congress for Cultural Freedom that stood against authoritarian regimes, like that of Batista, but by 1957, with more violence facing the nation, many

30 Rafael Rojas, *Viajes al saber: Ensayos sobre lectura y traducción en Cuba* (Leiden: Almenara, 2018), 118.
31 See Cairo, ed. "La polémica Mañach-Lezama-Vitier-Ortega," 91-130.
32 Marta Rojas, "El Moncada y La Historia me absolverá. La victoria de un revés," *Revista de la Biblioteca Nacional José Martí*, julio-diciembre 2003, 17-42.
33 Rigoberto Segreo and Margarita Segura, *Más allá del mito. Jorge Mañach y la revolución cubana* (Santiago de Cuba: Editorial Oriente, 2013).
34 Mañach, Preface to "La historia me absolverá," *La Jiribilla*, December 5-11, 2009, http://epoca2.lajiribilla.cu/2009/n448_12/448_02.html#_ftn2.

of its members left the island.[35] In 1959, Mañach returned to Cuba and taught at a private Catholic university. With enthusiasm toward the new leader and the revolution's policies, he published "El ángel de Fidel," in *Diario de la Marina* on April 4, 1959, and recently re-published in the compilation entitled *La cura que quisimos* (The cure we wanted).[36] In this essay can be seen Mañach's belief in the revolution's commitment to the rectification of Cuban life and its "proscription of venality, frivolity and irresponsibility,"[37] issues significant to Mañach since "The Crisis of High Culture" and *An Inquiry into Choteo*. In November 1960, in discord with the revolution, Mañach departed for Puerto Rico and taught at the University of San Juan in Rio Piedras. It is there that he wrote *La teoría de la frontera* (posthumously published and translated into English with the title *Frontiers in the Americas: A Global Perspective, 1975)*, that reflects upon, among other issues, the North's and the South's idiosyncratic psychologies and what he mistakenly saw as a "substantial change in the policy of the United States toward Latin America and toward Puerto Rico in particular,"[38] that could be propitious for Puerto Rico to be "a field for experimentation in the new order of inter-American relations

35 Patrick Iber, *Neither Peace nor Freedom: The Cultural Cold War in Latin America* (Cambridge: Harvard UP, 2015), 126. See Jorge Domingo Cuadriello, "La Asociación Cubana del Congreso por la Libertad de la Cultura," *Espacio Laical* 4 (2010): 78-82.

36 Jorge Mañach, *La cura que quisimos: Artículos sobre la Revolución Cubana*, ed. Carlos Espinosa (Richmond: Casa Vacía, 2018).

37 Mañach, "El ángel de Fidel," *La Jiribilla*, May 12-18, 2007, http://epoca2.lajiribilla.cu/2007/n314_05/314_31.html.

38 Jorge Mañach, *Frontiers in the Americas: A Global Perspective*, translated by Philip H. Phenix (New York: Teachers College Press, 1970), 90.

grounded in the freedom and dignity of all."[39] Mañach died in June of 1961.

On Translating Mañach

While Mañach's writings are important in Cuban studies, little of Mañach has appeared in English, only *Martí, El apóstol* (1933, *Martí: Apostle of Freedom*, 1950) and *Frontiers in the Americas: A Global Perspective*. The fact that he is a difficult figure to pin down, textually and ideologically across his life, is part of my own motivation to carry out this translation of one of the most authoritative essays in Spanish, comparable to other classic meditations on Latin American and national identity such as José Martí's "Nuestra América" (1891, English 1977), José Enrique Rodó's *Ariel* (1900, English 1988), José Carlos Mariátegui's *Seven Interpretive Essays on Peruvian Reality* (1928, English 1971), Antonio S. Pedreira's *Insularismo: An Insight into the Puerto Rican Character* (1934, English 2007), Samuel Ramos's *Profile of Man and Culture in Mexico* (1934, English 1962), and Octavio Paz's *The Labyrinth of Solitude* (1950, English 1962), among others. In addition to Mañach's curious rhetorical devices and logic that might be limiting factors for Mañach's academic cooption, it is likely that Mañach's political stances have also contributed to his problematic "use value" among academics.

I began the translation of *Indagación del choteo* with a small seminar of undergraduate students in 2015 as an exercise in collaborative translation. The inspiration for working with such a group on translation came from translator and scholar Esther Allen, while it was Ariana Hernandez-Reguant who convinced me of the urgency for doing so.

39 *Frontiers*, 93-94.

In fact, both visited the undergraduate seminar; Allen, to discuss Mañach's depiction of Cuba's founding father José Martí in *Martí, Apostle of Freedom,* and Hernandez-Reguant, to reflect upon the broader ramifications of choteo in Cuban theater. Undergraduates at the time—Christina Bauman, Morgan Handy, Kevin Johnston, Sonja Nishku, and Jacqueline Slemp—beautifully initiated the process of translation over the semester. Some of the seminar's most successful moments entailed the introduction by one of our university's librarians, Marisol Ramos, to certain digital tools such as the *ngram viewer,* that helped us to map the usage of certain words and phrases during distinct time periods and locate comparable ones in English. At other times, that technique was insufficient to trace the meaning of more obscure phrases such as "cosas Pacheco," whose imperviousness only a specialist in Mañach and the *vanguardia* of the caliber of Ana Cairo, could help us. As a class, our contemporary distance from Mañach's haughty register was perversely pleasurable to mimic in English. I believe that such ambivalent feelings—the combination of dislike and like that Mañach had toward his object of study and ours toward Mañach, our occasional feeling of out-of-synchness with his observations, and our desire to transport that ambiguous register into the target language—had intellectual value for us in the classroom, and continue to have value for readers especially interested in comparative discussions of race, class, and humor.

In fact, the project was ambitious for the allotted time period. So, over these years, *An Inquiry into Choteo* has necessitated my absorbing its meaning within its own context and style in order to conjure up an adequate tone for today's United States. That said, passages, like the following, from the author's note, published in the 1955 edition of the essay, could initially dissuade even the most interested of readers.

> Tal vez sigan conservando validez, sin embargo, mis observaciones sobre los rasgos peculiares y más estables de la psicología cubana. En determinada época, ellos proveyeron los mecanismos propicios para el tipo de expansión o de reacción que el choteo representó y que, con menos ubicuidad, representa todavía.
>
> However, perhaps my observations of the peculiar and more stable features of the Cuban psychology still hold true. Back then, they provided the mechanisms that enabled the kind of expansion or reaction that choteo represented and, to a lesser extent, still represents.

If I were Mañach's editor, I might suggest fewer words or substituting "they" for a more clear subject, but what would doing so imply? Do those enabling mechanisms really need to appear in the English and what about the "expansion" or "reaction" that choteo represented? How would eliminating them in favor of a simpler construction transform our understanding of Mañach's mindset? I postulate that some of these rhetorical strategies are related to Mañach's intellectual wavering as he approaches the subject matter, and therefore, I resist the urge to edit them for simplicity within English. Sometimes, however, Mañach simply chooses slightly peculiar phrasing in Spanish over ready-made expressions. In those cases, I search for the equivalent in English.

Not entirely detached from the issue of syntax is another issue that requires a little introduction: that is, the untranslatability of the terms "*parejería*" and "*gracia*." The first—

parejería—is a term that, as I became better acquainted with it, got further from targeting in English, for numerous reasons, which included my attempting to get a hold of its transforming usage throughout time. In *El habla popular cubana de hoy* (1985), Argelio Santisteban defines "parejería" as a person who "pretends to behave in a manner that does not correspond to his condition, the child who wants to act like an adult, the old person who believes he is young, and the person who is inexperienced who poses as knowledgeable."[40] Evidently, "parejería" has its more and less benign connotations. Lexicoon.org, a fascinating dictionary with examples of usage, definitions, synonyms, translations, and instances of words' appearances in books and in news, does not actually translate "parejería," though it does produce a diagram of related terms and, like the ngram viewer, registers the start of its usage around 1895. The ngram viewer directs us to a google book search where the term appears more frequently in Cuba (soon after the island's abolition of slavery in 1886) and the Caribbean, than it does in the rest of the Spanish-speaking world.

To Roberto González Echevarría's assertion that Mañach could be accused of "not studying the African presence seriously in his essay,"[41] something that Mañach critiques other Cuban scholars for not having done, I would emphasize that the question remains central to his anxious outline of Cuban identity. While, on the one hand, he affirms within a footnote that blacks provide "solemnity, seriousness, and respect" to the Cuban culture, their comportment is also buried within the history of the term

40 Argelio Santisteban, *El habla popular cubana de hoy* (Havana: Editorial de Ciencias Sociales, 1985), 370.
41 Roberto González Echevarría, *Cuban Fiestas* (New Haven: Yale University Press, 2010), digital edition.

parejería that, as we shall see, Mañach, likewise, reveals within a footnote. The dramatization of how whites perceived blacks in Cuba trying to behave in an equivalent manner to whites is at the core of *teatro bufo* (theater of the buffoon/ blackface theater) of the nineteenth century, in such plays as Francisco Fernández Vilarós's *Los negros catedráticos* (1868), and is alluded to with the phrase "negro parejero" in a well-known Cuban popular song from 1882, "El negro José Caliente." In *Cuba*/España, *España/ Cuba* (1995), Manuel Moreno Fraginals renders the related term *"emparejamiento"* stating, "to be like whites was a form of social climbing, of achieving respect and consideration from white society."[42] In a crucial footnote within the text that does not appear in every edition of the essay in Spanish, Mañach notes:

> Here I'm restoring what appears to be the primary meaning of this word that is so much ours. In effect, it has come to assume, by derivation, that of "person who puts on airs, who considers himself superior," an attitude that is contrary to egalitarianism. Nevertheless, that meaning comes from the same idea of presumption that was associated with the word when primarily it was employed, as is well-known, to designate individuals of color who conducted themselves as white, who "caught up with/made himself equal to" him.

In the famous 1937 poem, "Prelude in Boricua," by Puerto Rican Luis Palés Matos, Julio Marzán translated "parejero" as "uppity." Pales Matos's verses begin: "Tuntun de pasa y griferia/ y otros parejeros tuntunes." Marzán translates

42 Manuel Moreno Fraginals, *Cuba/España, España/Cuba* (Barcelona: Crítica, Grijalbo Mondadori, 1995), 185.

these verses as, "Tomtom of kinky hair and black things/ and other uppity tomtoms."[43] While "uppityness" and "parejería" both speak to the intersections of race and class and the notion of stepping out of one's station, the different histories of African-descended people, of slavery and of the color/class structures in the United States and Cuba would problematize envisioning "parejería" and "uppityness" as identical. Furthermore, Mañach's footnote already points to the fact that Cubans themselves had already lost sight of the "primary meaning" of "parejería." In contrast, in today's United States, at least, "uppity" tends to pertain to race. The first time, for instance, that Mañach employs "parejería," he does so without that detailed explanation and uses it in a way to connote an overly familiar behavior—a usage that "uppityness" could not fulfill.

One instance of the relationship between choteo and parejería is clearly elaborated by Armando Valdés Zamora. He exemplifies a visual representation of choteo in Víctor Patricio Landaluze's famous nineteenth century painting *José Francisco*, depicting a black house slave kissing the lips of a white aristocratic woman on a bust. He observes the slave secretly making himself equivalent to the social and carnal world of his masters, while spectators and the artist make fun of his "parejero" act. For Valdés Zamora,

What defines choteo, in the way that Jorge Mañach presents it, is implicit in those two simultaneous gestures in the painting: to be equal to someone of superior authority, to desacralize through humor the emblems of that authority, and to judge

43 Cecilia Vicuña and Ernesto Livón-Grossman, eds. *The Oxford Book of Latin American Poetry: A Bilingual Anthology* (New York: Oxford University Press, 2009), 195-196.

those who do it without possessing the social attributes that correspond to them. *Chotear* is in this way synonymous with to depreciate the serious representation of individuals and their way of speaking.[44]

While racial connotations around the term *parejería* appear to have faded in Cuba over time, the politics of whitening mainstream Cuban thought have not been abolished. As Enrique del Risco succinctly notes, parejería "emerged in the colonial context when domestic slaves attempted to speak and behave like their master,"[45] and although by the second half of the twentieth century, calling someone "parejero" was used with endearment, discussions of the structures of racism around Cuba continue to ignite fiery debates, making a renewed discussion of *An Inquiry into Choteo* within a comparative context crucial.

21st Century Associations

Ideology, race, and class are connected in the Cuban imagination through complex histories that frequently reside in the nation's footnotes. Despite the fact that today's United States is removed from the particular postcolonial and neocolonial Cuban experience that informed *An Inquiry into Choteo* and that it continues to take pride in political correctness and egalitarianism, the first few decades of the twenty-first century United States are a hotbed of racial and

44 Armando Valdéz Zamora, "Una lectura de la sátira en Cuba: Indagación del choteo de Jorge Mañach," *La balsa de la musa*, October 18, 2014, http://labalsadelamusa.over-blog.com/2014/10/una-lectura-de-la-satira-en-cuba-indagacion-del-choteo-de-jorge-manach.html.
45 I initiated this conversation on my facebook page on October 5, 2016, asking "how might you translate 'parejería' into english?"

class tensions. I introduce the comparison, as I believe that, as a U.S. American, whose homeland has been in a long, slow war with Cuba, it is essential to think about issues regarding Cuba in a comparative fashion. The U.S.-Cuban problem is one that cannot be solved through geopolitical maneuverings such as "normalization," alone, but rather with studying the intricacies of relationships that emerge, in such texts as Mañach's *An Inquiry into Choteo.*

In March 2016, Barack Obama visited Cuba, the first U.S. president to meet with Cuban officials on the island since 1928. Celebratory and critical portraits of the former president and his family abounded. Some of the impressions he left on Cubans that are not necessarily encountered in the press, but are in everyday life, pertained to Obama's "gracia," that way about him that made him familiar to them. One echo of that notion can be found in the comments section of Fernando Ravsberg's blog in which, after praising Obama's speech and his overall intentions, a commentator states "besides the black guy is an excellent orator and actor, because part of his gracia is natural."[46] "Grace and class" are actually two words that pervade the most favorable of journalistic impressions of Barack and Michelle Obama in the U.S. press, as well. The former president even praised his wife for her "grace and grit," a turn on the frequently-used phrase to identify the couple, in one of the most emotional moments of his final speech as president.

46 "además el negro es excelente orador y actor, porque parte de la gracia es actuación natural" in Fernando Ravsberg, "El discurso de Obama fue brillante y eficaz de cara al cubano medio," *Cartas desde Cuba: Comments,* March 22, 2016, http://cartasdesdecuba. com/el-discurso-de-obama-fue-brillante-y-eficaz-de-cara-al-cubano-medio.

Warm and sometimes, overly intimate expressions of how many Cuban people felt at the time toward Obama, however, went hand and hand with its "choteada" version, evidenced in the controversial headline "Negro, tú eres sueco?" (Black guy, are you Swedish). The article was authored by Elias Argudín, published in *Tribuna de la Habana*, on March 27, 2016.[47] The phrase, anything but obscure in Cuba, is utilized here by a journalist of color to undermine through choteo the vision of Cuba toward which Obama was urging the Cuban people to move. Michael J. Bustamante accurately sums up Argudín's use of the joke:

A reference to a comedy sketch from the 1980s, in which an Afro-Cuban attempts to pass himself off as a Swedish diplomat to buy goods sold only to foreigners in special stores, the joke appeared to question the veracity of Obama's blackness. A real black man, the article insinuated, should know better than to preach or believe in the merits of U.S. political 'freedoms' that allow "(white) policeman to massacre at will any Afro-descendent."[48]

Obama's speech at the national theater was thus discounted by Argudín, in his attempt to elucidate Cuban official discrepancy with Obama's diplomacy, once again illustrating

---

47 Elias Argudín, "Negro, ¿tú eres sueco?" *Tribuna de la Habana*, March 24, 2016, http://www.tribuna.cu/opinion/2016-03-24/negro-eres-sueco#comment-4934.
48 Michael J. Bustamante, "Review of Devyn Spence Benson's *Antiracism in Cuba: The Unfinished Revolution*," *NACLA Report on the Americas* 48.2 (2016): 296.

why continued attention to the problems set forth by Mañach is important.

In addition to the speech, the Cuban people also got to know Obama, doing his own joking around, through his appearance in skits on one of the most popular Cuban comedy shows, *Vivir del cuento*. And yet, with all of Obama's grace and humor, he is still perceived "officially" as a black guy who has stepped out of bounds, a sense that, I might add, is pervasive within the United States, where it is less easy to qualify such dimensions in terms of "official" discourse. "Gracia," while simpler than parejería, is another word that somewhat confounds translation of Mañach's essay, since, while in English "grace" and gratitude are linked and can refer to both God's beneficence as well as a kind of simple elegance, in Spanish, grace's link to levity and humor is also preserved. After much deliberation, working with my students and provisionally thinking of "gracia" as "comedic gift," I decided to leave "gracia" in Spanish.

For Mañach, that Cuban comedic gift can be, in fact, closely linked to choteo. And yet, Mañach suggests that gracia relates to a "certain disposition and clarity of mind, the kind that everything bounces off, without penetrating, without leaving any trace." He then associates "this form of optimism that smooth[s] over the edges of reality" as "predominantly feminine." Curiously, this explanation of gracia is one of the only moments that Mañach comments upon women directly in his analysis, where the feminine realm is not merely the "other" to "the Cuban" (man), but part of the actual object of analysis. Nevertheless, the phrase "el cubano" is not proper to Mañach, but rather, common usage among Cubans. While I did deliberate over changing "el cubano" to "Cubans," much more characteristic of contemporary English, I ultimately decided not to neutralize the phrase in order preserve the subtle shifts in Mañach's positionality, his emphasis on the specificity of his subject, as well as mark this exceptional moment in which Mañach names the "feminine" in relation to gracia.

If parejería could be contained, would choteo, in fact, move closer to gracia? Or might practitioners be subjected to a different kind of vigilance? An excess of gracia could be perceived as slippery. In fact, it may spill over into parejería. *An Inquiry into Choteo* continues to fascinate, not solely within the Cuban context, but on the transatlantic spectrum, which even takes into account the United States whose histories of miscegenation were distinct from those of the Spanish, Portuguese, and French colonies, but where issues of diversity and class have hardy vanished.

Jacqueline Loss

Inquiry into Choteo

By Jorge Mañach

Author's Note

The two previous editions of this essay, first delivered as a lecture in 1928, have been sold out for a long time. I am pleased to publish it now in its third edition with the Editorial Libro Cubano—a nice new venture that deserves our support.

Although I do not enjoy fiddling with old writings of mine, this time it seems fitting to do so, trimming parts here and there to remove excess, clarifying some concepts and adding a brief note, from today's perspective (1955), that considers the extent to which we have already "moved beyond" *choteo* as a habit or a generalized attitude.

However, perhaps my observations of the peculiar and more stable features of the Cuban psychology still hold true. Back then, they provided the mechanisms that enabled the kind of expansion or reaction that choteo represented and, to a lesser extent, still represents.

J.M.

In Defense of the Trivial

Perhaps the topic of this lecture seems strange to some of you. It may not seem serious.

This matter of seriousness, however, is precisely what is going to occupy a bit of our attention today. The concept of seriousness is itself extremely vague. Many things taken seriously turn out, upon rigorous examination, to be undeserving of this category; they are Pacheco[1] things. And, on the contrary, there are things that hide their essential importance behind a trivial and laughable exterior, such as those men who walk the earth with the soul of an amphora inside the body of a jug.

The same things happen to ideas. Certain time periods have displayed a marked tendency to coat basically fatuous ideas with gravity. For example, the last century, owing to its romantic exaltation and almost superstitious devotion to "principles," inflated numerous concepts, ascribing them with real content and transcendence that subsequent eras were forced to deny. Until now, those overblown ideas enjoyed an enviable prestige of superiority. Modern realism has injected them with irony, depriving them of what

---

1   T.N. "Pacheco things" refer to the triumphs of the inept. It is a reference to Portuguese writer José Maria Eça de Queirós's discussion of the Pacheco character in *Correspondence of Fradique Mendes*, originally published in 1900, in which an average person rises to fame and success in a foolish society although he or she is undeserving of such a feat. Cubans were familiar with his writing, in part because Eça de Queirós was a consul stationed in Havana between 1872 and 1873. Ana Cairo, E-mail message to author, February 27, 2015.

in *criollo*[2] we call their "*vivío*."[3] This same time period of ours, antagonistic to all that is serious, insists on vindicating the importance of what was once considered despicable and strives to discover the meaning of the insignificant. Topics have been renewed with the preeminence granted by our time to plain ideas. The highest authorities urge us to aban-

2   T.N. It is generally believed that "criollo," during the Colonial Period in the Americas, meant a child of Spaniards who was born in Cuba. Yet even before the 16th century, in Cuba, "criollo" also referred to those who were born in Cuba, irrespective of their origins in Europe or Africa. See Tato Quiñones, "Negro, negro criollo, afrocubano, afrodescendiente," *Negra cubana tenía que ser*, September 9, 2014, https://negracubanateniaqueser.com/2014/09/09/negro-negro-criollo-afrocubano-afrodescendiente. Today, it also refers to the mixture that appears as inherent to Cuba. Here, the author is referring to Cubans' language and way of speaking, although frequently, the author uses it as synonymous with "Cuban."

3   T.N. I have decided to keep "vivío" in the original criollo (or Cuban Spanish) since Mañach is calling attention to a Cuban word that was common during his lifetime. In a lecture given at the Club Atenas in Havana on May 15, 1942 and at the Centro de Estudios Superiores in the Oriente province between August 25 and August 28, 1944, Elías Entralgo gave a lecture entitled "La liberación étnica cubana: el fenómeno mulato" (Cuban Ethnic Liberation: The Mulatto Phenomenon) in which he states: "El *vivío*, que es irse sosteniendo económicamente, estirar la subsistencia, sin grandes preocupaciones de adelanto colectivo ni siquiera personal, sino mediante algún acomodo que resuelva cierto número de necesidades con el menor esfuerzo posible. Representativos extremados del vivío son el vividor y el que vive del cuento, aquel más común y éste más raro." (The *vivío*, which is going about sustaining oneself economically, stretching subsistence, without major concerns for collective or even personal advancement, but rather through some arrangement that resolves a certain number of necessities with the least amount of effort. Extreme representatives of *vivío* are the scrounger and he who lives by his wits, the former more common than the latter.) Elías Entralgo, *La liberación étnica cubana* (Havana: University of Havana, 1953), 201.

don Olympian curiosities and observe the small and familiar things, the humble things, that are around us.

This is of vital interest. Our existence must border on the minute and immediate, which constitutes our circumstance, our surroundings. But since the minute and immediate is so common and close to us, we mistakingly think we already understand it. We do not look at our own environment from the outside enough, remarks Christopher Morley; we do not look at it with the curiosity that we ought to. Therefore we have to apply ourselves to the inquiry into the multitude of trifles through which we constitute our lives.

When it comes to psychological and relational facts, like choteo, scrutiny can have a surprising sociological scope. Georg Simmel has already stressed the benefit of introducing the microscopic method into sociology, "applying the principle of infinitely many and infinitely small effects, juxtaposed on society, as in the sciences of juxtaposition."[4] Instead of studying society through cumbersome abstractions, we shall explore it in its minute concretions, in its small, vital modules.

Choteo—something familiar, slight, and festive—is a form of relating that we consider typically Cuban, and that is already reason enough for us to investigate its nature, keeping in mind our social psychology. Although its importance is something that has come at a great cost, with pessimistic overtones, since Cuba reached the age of reason, no Cuban critic I know of has decided to investigate, with any degree of detail, the causes and consequences of such a regrettable

4   Jorge Simmel, *Sociología* (Madrid: Editorial Revista de Occidente 1927), 30. T.N. English translation from George Simmel. *Sociology: Inquiries into the Construction of Social Forms*, translated by Anthony J. Blasi, Anton Jacobs, and Mathew Kanjirathinkal (Leiden: Brill, 2009), 33-34.

psychosocial phenomenon. Partly on account of our era's fondness for large topics, and partly due to our habit of resolving problems with mere allusions, the few Cuban books that deal with our psychology, at most, have settled for just a passing allusion to the subject of choteo. Because this vernacular name has almost always been avoided, the peculiarities of the phenomenon have been ignored, and choteo has been confused with other, more generic qualities of the criollo character, like "levity," "cheerfulness," and the like.[5] Here is also where our confusion takes hold.

That very lack of previous exploration complicates an initial investigation—already arduous for how tenuous the common concept of choteo is and for the variety of attitudes and situations that it appears to reference. What method would allow us to penetrate with some certainty into a psychic and evasive social experience that is so elusive, so multiform, and not at all concrete?

Of course, this is a question of discerning the meaning of the word "choteo." But here lies a problem of semantics, in which etymology, such a valuable aid in the science of meanings, does not help us. There has been much speculation into the origin of the word. There are Andalusians who wanted to link it to the word "*choto*," which is a name given in Spain, and in that region, in particular, to the baby goat. The verb "*chotar*"—from the Latin "*suctare*"—means "to suckle" and by extension "to behave with the lack of dig-

5   T.N. With minor changes, I have *almost* wholly extracted from Gustavo Pérez Firmat's excellent translation of this fragment, beginning with "the few books" and ending with "cheerfulness," which appears in *Literature and Liminality: Festive Readings in the Hispanic Tradition* (Durham: Duke, 1986), 71.

nity" exhibited by suckling kids.[6] Choteo, therefore, would be behaving like a baby goat. Clearly, this derivation is not impossible. It is also not impossible that the word "choteo" belongs to the very considerable body of African words that have become naturalized in our criollo jargon. But not even the illustrious Fernando Ortiz, authority in the Afro-Cuban province of our sociology, is very sure of himself regarding the African etymon, venturing only to make possible links with the Lucumi term "*soh*" or "*chot*," which involves the idea of conversing, and to the Pongüe "*chota*," which denotes the act of spying. Obviously, this last connection would lend itself to explaining the employment of the term *choteo* as it has come to be used in Cuba, in the sense of accusation or denunciation, but it does not shed any light on the meaning of choteo as a jocular attitude. In any case, the etymology can only serve as a starting point for an inquiry into the meanings when it is unquestionable, when it offers a definitive root for grounding the spirit of our findings.

Given the failure of the etymological method, we seem to have no other means of tackling choteo than to grasp the common concept: to see the definition that is usually given to it, to abstractly study the logical implications of that definition, and to compare them later with objective

6   Regarding these derivations, don Miguel de Unamuno wrote me to acknowledge having received my essay: "In support of the etymology of *choto*, little kid, note *cabrear*. In Spain it is said, that they got him *cabreado* when bothered, fed up with mockery." Although the rest of Unamuno's letter does not have much to do with the topic of this essay, I'll publish the complete text in the appendix because everything by this great Spaniard ought to be preserved in print. (J.M., 1939). T.N. This note and appendix was published in the first, in the 1940 edition, as well in the Mnemosyne edition published in Miami in 1969. I have included this note, but not the appendix, because it continues to support the importance Unamuno held for Mañach.

observations. Thus, in combining an empirical method with a logical one, we shall simultaneously elude the dangers of excessive abstractions and incomplete experiences.

An Initial Definition

If we were to ask the average Cuban, the Cuban "on the street," to tell us what he understands to be choteo, he would give us a simplistic version. However, this would be fairly close to a definition because it would logically imply everything that we have found contained in the most typical manifestations of the phenomenon. Choteo, he would say, consists of "not taking anything seriously." We can still press our point a bit further, and he would clarify it for us—using a phrase that is not usually said in front of ladies, so I ask you to mention it as little as possible—he would clarify for us that choteo consists of "tirarlo todo a *relajo*."[7]

As you can see, these two versions that the average informant gives us coincide, so far, in assigning choteo an absolutist and systematic, so to speak, nature. We label a politician "a systematic opposer" when he makes a habit out of opposing without caring much whether the objects of his opposition are really reprehensible. Similarly the *choteador*[8] takes everything as a joke and apparently does not grant importance to anything. He is a kind of professional at that attitude, and now, we shall see that, to the choteador, it doesn't even matter whether the objects or situations being mocked are truly worthy of laughter. Choteo is then an al-

---

7   T.N. "Tirarlo a *relajo*" or "tirar a relajo," as Mañach later refers to this phrase, means to make fun of everything. I have chosen to keep "relajo" in the Spanish original most of the times Mañach uses it, because of the context Mañach provides for it. The point that such slang is not usually uttered in the presence of women is especially fascinating since women are only mentioned in rare instances in this essay. "Relajo," an important aspect of choteo, according to Mañach, is a kind of letting it all down.

8   T.N. "*Choteador*" refers to someone who utilizes choteo.

titude hardened into a habit, and this habitualness is its most important characteristic.

Before specifying what the attitude consists of, we must carefully establish its limits. When it is said that choteo does not take "anything" seriously, or that "everything" is turned into a joke, it is evident that those words, "anything" and "everything" are used hyperbolically; that is to say, that they are not true to the letter, even though they are true in a general sense. What is suggested in an emphatic way is that choteo does not *take anything seriously that is generally taken to be serious*. And it is still necessary to limit this category of facts even further because the most jocular man can only take certain things seriously whose seriousness is not a matter of opinion, for example, a toothache. During a cyclone, I watched as some neighbors cracked up amidst the havoc until a big gust of wind removed the roof of their own house. Likewise, choteo systematically maintains its attitude toward all things taken seriously so long as they do not affect it in such a way that would make using choteo impossible.

That said, in the abstract, of what does the action *"chotear"*[9] consist? We shall see that the two aforementioned definitions point to the same external fact—a habit of irreverence—motivated by the same psychological fact: a repugnance toward all authority.

In effect, to take seriously is the equivalent of conducting oneself respectfully toward something. Because, as we know, respect does not necessarily mean compliance. The same Latin etymology (*respicere*: to look again) reveals the exact sense of the word, which is that of careful consideration, that of regard. An opinion that we consider erroneous

9   T.N. The verb "chotear" refers to using choteo.

can be respected. We speak about "human respect" which, according to religion, is often contrary to the interests of the spirit. We also speak of respect toward children. Respect, therefore, is nothing more than painstaking attention, and a lack of respect is even, colloquially, *a lack of attention.* We do not take things seriously when we do not pay them sustained or sufficiently undivided attention. So, the hastily impressionable man, the extroverted man, or the man of wandering curiosity, is generally a disrespectful man, a great candidate for choteo.

Of course, at the core of respect, there is always an idea of authority, present or potential, which invites our attention. If we respect a ruler, it is because we know he can ultimately exercise a physical dominance over us. Respect for the man of knowledge or for the righteous man is based on an appreciation of his preeminence, of his intellectual or moral authority. Societal respect is an homage to the authority of numbers and the opinion of others. Respect for children, for the weak, is a tribute to humanity and, like religion, masks a vague feeling of dependence. In the same vein, a chronic lack of respect can also originate from *an absence of a sense of authority,* either because the individual excessively declares his personal value and his will or because he reacts to a social environment in which hierarchy has been lost or falsified. "Tirar a relajo" serious things is, therefore, no more than ignoring, at least in a superficial way, the element of authority that is or could be in them, to create an atmosphere of debauchery around them.

An Inner Assessment

These first conclusions allow us to suggest a solution to the problem that is posed regarding the choteador's psychic attitude. It is evident that not taking anything seriously does not necessarily mean that the existence of serious things is ignored or denied, deep down, but rather that, upon acknowledging them, a disrespectful attitude toward them is also adopted. What matters then is to find out the degree of esteem that exists deep inside choteo: whether the choteador admits to himself that there are serious things and does not revere them, or whether his behavior results instead from his not finding anything serious in the world. In the first case, choteo would be merely a vice of behavior; in the second, a vice of mental outlook or moral sensibility.

Upon scrutinizing diverse individual cases of choteo that we come across, we note that individuals exist among us who are incapable of being respectful in any situation, who even *admit* that nothing merits respect. Equipped almost invariably with a very basic upbringing, whatever their exterior decorum, they ignore all the deeds and feats of the spirit; hardened toward sensitivity, they neither perceive what is sublime or what is revered in the physical or human order. These are the professional nay-sayers, disbelievers to the extreme, the all-out egoists, who cannot access any serious emotion outside the range of animals. They have, as Gracián said, "sinister wit," and when you talk to them about fatherland, home, integrity, or culture, they crack a joke, and they tell you that all those things are merely "romanticism." The customary language and attitudes of these kinds of men are those of choteo.

But at their side, mingling with them, we find other individuals who are just as ready to be facetious when it comes to more serious matters and even in situations most demanding of circumspection. Nevertheless, it is enough to explore them using suggestive dialectical reasoning, which captures their attention and sympathy, to discover that behind their frivolity and skepticism, they are hiding a soul as sensitive and gullible as a child's. Also, while their speech and habitual attitude are those of choteo, once in a while they exhibit a dormant sensitivity and a rusty aptitude for forming affirmative value judgments.

Which of these two types of choteadores represent the true choteo?

We are faced with a phenomenon too fluid and variable to strictly conform to either of these rigid categories. Given that we only know choteo as an external attitude, we cannot speak out about its content with certainty. What seems more certain is that there is a light, healthy choteo that is almost purely exterior. This is mainly due to the vices or lack of attention derived from this same criollo psychology. Then there is another choteo that is more cutting and skeptical, maybe a perversion of the previous one, originating in a genuine breakdown in the sense of authority that we analyzed previously.

For the moment, let's set aside having to decide which of these two kinds of choteo is the most widespread and genuine, and now try to outline the social morphology that is common to both types of choteo, their peculiar ways of occurring.

Choteo in the Hierarchy of Mockery

As such, it seems clear that both types of choteo, the skeptical and the merely jocular, translate into a form of mockery that may be more or less explicit, more or less referring to an external situation or to a value judgment.

That said, mockery is an essentially human trait. Mere laughter has always been held as one of the exclusive powers of man. For a very long time many have said that humans are the only animals that laugh and, apparently, in accordance with that postulate, Bergson, a great modern philosopher, discovered very important biological and social implications of that "human" faculty. Laughter could be something like a "social gesture" of protest against the mechanization of life: our species' act of foresight.

Those of us who have briefly observed the most expressive of animals—a dog or a monkey, for example—can harbor some doubts about this supposed human monopoly on laughter, at least with regard to its most intrinsic claim. If anything, what is exclusive to humans is the type of expression they make when externalizing a state of euphoria, jubilation, or pleasant anticipation. What is, in fact, a propensity peculiar to humans is mockery. The parrot and the monkey, among others, seem capable of ridicule, but in all probability theirs is a simple mimicry devoid of genuine intention.

Whether or not accompanied by laughter, mockery, strictly speaking, is a human and social activity, whose instinctive purpose is to affirm one's own individuality against another's that is considered superior or equally powerful. *All mockery assumes a position of authority, or at least competence.* Because of this, mocking a child, a sick person, or an elderly person is unreasonable and instinctively disgusts us. They are weak; there's no need to attack them. Mockery is an act of subterfuge before the fort; no wonder that mocking, in a sense, is synonymous with evading. Human instinct tends to preserve our independence, our freedom to adapt, and it is suspicious of all authority, including the authority of prestige which, as Simmel already observed, entraps us perhaps more than any other type.

With regard to that power of mockery as a central concept, a hierarchy or scale of social reactions is produced that begins with the purely instinctive expression of children toward their parents, or toward their teacher and, from parody to satire to irony, they reach the most elevated kind of humor. At this superior level, the element of mockery is so subtle that it is hardly noticeable and even seems like a delicate form of solidarity and respect.

Mockery differs from all other forms of protest and precautionary measures against authority in that it stands up against what is comical or, in other words, self-contradictory, about authority. Pointing out that contradiction, it aims to undermine the authority that exhibits it. Therefore mockery is more elevated and more effective the more refined its discernment of this contradiction; and, in contrast, it is cruder the closer it gets to the mere instinctive protest of a child, because it focuses on what is outwardly comical about authority or because it attributes something comical to it that it does not have, like when school children pin the tail on their teacher's coat.

Therefore, if it is discernment or some critical sense that situates those reactions as higher or lower within the hierarchy of mockery, it can be clearly inferred that choteo, as a habit, as a systematic attitude that it is, generally turns out to be a very low form of mockery. Where no one has grounds for laughter, the choteador finds them or pretends to find them. That would have to be due either to a greater perspicacity on the part of choteo to discern what is comical about authority or the assumption of something comical where there isn't any.

Choteo's superior insight into what is comical about the authoritarian realm is, at times, undeniable. The average Cuban, like all peoples around the world with quick mental abilities, obviously has a sense of humor. If, as a rule, he is not particularly deep, he is able to immediately perceive all superficial aspects of any fact and swiftly implement the mental pathways leading toward the comic spark. As a result, at times, choteo does have true *gracia*[10]: it discovers for us the laughable objective that had gone unnoticed by the most intense observers or those with less mental agility.

However, often choteo doesn't reveal anything really funny at all. A joke, whatever kind of wit, provokes laughter anytime, anywhere; choteo, instead, is strictly conditioned by time and space. We are rarely amused by someone else's retelling of an instance of choteo in which we have not participated; instead, what usually happens is that the tale irritates us. This is not due to a lack of that feeling of solidarity that, according to Bergson, a laughable experience requires, but rather to the fact that, in those cases, choteo seems like mockery without a motive. Even worse, as mockery that in-

10 T.N. After much deliberation, and with the encouragement of one of University of Connecticut's librarians, Marisol Ramos, *gracia* will remain in Spanish. While in English, grace and gratitude are linked, they can refer to a virtue from God and also to a kind of simple elegance. In Spanish, grace's link to levity and, in addition, to humor is preserved. Eventually, Mañach evokes all meanings, making the Spanish word "gracia" the most precise. I talk about this word more in my introduction to this essay.

vents its own motive, choteo *"pins the tail"*[11] on a serious object. It creates an atmosphere of jocularity around any respectable person or situation that rapidly gets more and more charged until it becomes so dense that the observed object seems disfigured and grotesque.

On occasion, this object-pretext doesn't even exist. How many times, at the theater or whatever sort of show, have we not seen a yawn, a jocular phrase without any relevance, launched randomly, colliding with the public's concentration and becoming the center of irradiation for growing waves of choteo? In these cases, what could be the reason behind this mockery without apparent purpose? What is the function of this aimless laughter? Perhaps, in order to explain it, it would be necessary to resort to that vague subsidiary aim of rest that Bergson attributed to it; or rather, to think that, on the contrary, in those moments, criollo laughter functions as an artificial stimulant with which we try to overcome the fatigue, the flattening, and the lassitude of the tropics. In any case, it is a fundamentally selfish and thoughtless act, by means of which the choteador seems to laugh just to be cheerful, as if to confirm William James's well-known theory of emotions: We do not cry because we are sad; we are sad because we cry.

Nevertheless, choteo would not be as dangerous as it generally is, if it were to limit itself to being that laughter without an object. Usually it does have an object, and that object is its victim. Perhaps even in those cases in which it looks like pure improvisation, it is really choteo reacting against something external, that not even it can detect well. In the

11 Mañach says "pone rabo," and says it is a "very meaningful criollo phrase." It means to laugh at a person behind her/his back, as in the game "pin the tail on the donkey."

example we put forth of the theater, the jocular phrase or the loud yawn is perhaps a sign of protest against something. A paper moth descending from paradise more likely carries in its beak a warlike intention than an olive branch. In other words, choteo almost always implies a state of impatience, a suspicion of some limitation. Maybe it is just about having to remain silent before a spectacle that is drawn out or bores the public, but it will always be the limitation imposed by a real or imagined authority.

Choteo and Order

This interpretation explains to us why choteo is the enemy of order in all its manifestations. Observe well any case or situation of choteo, and you will see that *it always entails elements of disorder*. For choteo to give rise to typical criollo mockery, it's important for it and characteristic of it not to entail any frustration of dignity.

The accident that undermines one's desire to behave circumspectly[12] has always been a laughing matter. It has already been said that no clown or comedian is comparable to certain fruit peels on the pavement. Some actors have taken a good look at this and learned how to take advantage of its possibilities. For instance, what is Charlie Chaplin's sublimely comical (that is to say, profoundly humorous) art, but a symphony in the key of frustrated dignity? What makes it so pathetically ridiculous to us is the ease with which a man who dons a suit, cane, and bowler hat becomes the victim of accidents.

Throughout the world, I repeat, accidents against dignity give rise to laughter, so uncontrollable, that it's almost like a reflex. Strictly speaking, it is based on instinct. It seems to obey that ancient and secret joy that we experience when we see fellow man—our competitor in the fight for life—facing opposition to his claim of hierarchy, of the importance of his own growth. This feeling is not, of course, foreign to choteo, because choteo includes all other elemental forms of mockery. But the disorder before which that very Cuban form of rejoicing typically occurs is no accident against dignity. *It is*

12 T.N. I have taken the translation "that undermines one's desire to behave circumspectly" from Gustavo Pérez Firmat, *Literature and Liminality*, 60.

the disorder that consists, purely and simply, in the altera-tion of any state of agreement and hierarchy, whether it be in the physical or objective realm.

Once a very criollo friend of mine, devoid of all intellectual malice although quite seasoned in other sorts, told me, in all earnest, his impressions of being aboard a steamboat during a storm. What seemed to impress him most was the displacement that the cargo, poorly secured in the bilge, suffered on account of the boat's lurches: "The barrels," he said, "the packages, boxes, everything was going from one side to another: the whole thing was a choteo."

In other words, choteo is confusion, subversion, disorder; in sum "relajo." So, what does this word mean but the relaxation of all the linkages and conjunctures that give things an articulated appearance, a dignified integrity? The fact that my friend used the word "choteo" to describe circumstances as unpleasant as those of a storm makes it even more significant. His metaphorical use of the word "choteo" does not lessen the possibility that a case of choteo could exist with no real cause for mockery or rejoicing. Mere disorder is not a thing that has gracia in itself. Choteo doesn't find gracia in it either, but when faced with this kind of situation, choteo takes pride in it *because it carries with it a negation of all hierarchy* that, for certain types of tropical idiosyncrasy, is always odious. All order implies some authority. Ordering is synonymous with commanding. In disorder, the individual can be more at ease. There is no outward composure that encourages keeping a corresponding personal composure. Orderliness imposes a kind of disciplinary exemplariness on one's spirit. There is nothing that makes me more uneasy than entering an office where everything is in order; instead, where things are a complete mess, I always experience a sense of familiarity. This desire for familiarity with things is something to which the Cuban is exceedingly addicted. We shall see that one of the determinant causes of choteo is the leveling tendency that characterizes us Cubans, that which we call *"parejería"*[13] and that leads us to say "old man" and "boy" to the most exalted or venerable man.

13 T.N. The word in Spanish is "parejería" and refers to a mode of behaving with excessive confidence or presumptuousness that entails speaking to all as if they were equals. In my introduction to this essay, I expound on this term a bit more, and, in addition, Mañach explains it in a footnote the second time he uses the word.

But first, what interests us is to examine how this penchant for disorder, this hatred of hierarchy that is an essential aspect of choteo, informs the most important manifestation of the phenomenon: its craving for devaluation. The conventional index of value is prestige. And prestige is, in effect, one of the forms of seriousness against which choteo takes a wholehearted stand: seriousness in reputation. In contrast, the "*choteado*" is that which has a precarious or false reputation: the smeared.

This manifestation of choteo is frequent among us. We often see the least "sophisticated" of Cubans, with regard to upbringing, call into question the most treasured of moral, intellectual, and even sentimental values. They convert a woman's virtue, a man's intellectual determination, the emotion elicited by a funeral or bereavement, into a laughing matter. Once, some Cubans visited the Municipal Crematorium in Paris. Upon seeing a corpse enter the incinerator, one of our compatriots exclaimed to the funeral operator, "Once over, please."[14] With questionable taste, but indisputable witticism, he reduced the human remains to the category of a steak. Taunts around wakes are classic among us. Choteo does not even respect the sacred presence of death.

When mockery is formed in opposition to any immediate quality or value, the characteristic feature of choteo is not one of skepticism or intentional satire. Many times, the choteador admires, deep down, the same virtue that he

14 T.N. "Once over," the translation of "de vuelta en vuelta" used by Pérez Firmat (*Literature and Liminality*, 57) means "medium rare." There, Pérez Firmat convincingly explains that "once over" maintains the quality of movement that is also entailed in *choteo*.

is mocking. And this raises an interesting question: could choteo in its devaluing form really be an expression of resentment?

Derived from Nietzsche and developed by Max Scheler, a well-known German theory exists, according to which resentment acts as an instigator and "definer of an entire morality." "We have a tendency," Max Scheler says, "to overcome any strong tension between desire and impotence by depreciating or denying the positive value of the desired object. At times, indeed, we go so far as to extol another object which is somehow opposed to the first."[15] This sentiment, so close to spite, explains numerous types of false assessments in modern life. Drawing from Scheler's own in-depth analysis, however, it is doubtful whether this sentiment can explain any form of mockery, since it is already a release and direct devaluation, whereas the judgment of resentment originates in repression and acts indirectly. At most, it could be said that certain types of envious mockery are—in the words of the same philosopher—the "discharge" that eliminates "that psychical dynamite that is called *ressentiment*."[16]

Undoubtedly, in many cases, choteo obeys this goal of discharge. But it is necessary to do it the justice of recognizing that, typically, neither rancor nor resentment is characteristic of it. This "can never emerge without the mediation of a particular form of impotence,"[17] and the choteador is not always incapable of assuming the same value that he ridicules. On the contrary. Our artful mocker is precisely

---

15 Max Scheler, *El resentimiento en lo moral*, trans. José Gaos (Madrid: Editorial Revista de Occidente, 1927), 69. T.N. Max Scheler, *Ressentiment*, trans. Louis A. Coser, 1915, www.mercaba.org/SANLUIS/Filosofia/autores/Contemporánea/Scheller/Ressentiment.pdf.
16 T.N. Scheler, 20.
17 T.N. Scheler, 15.

the one who laughs at the very values that he would emulate if he were to surrender to their servitude. As this is what precisely feels unpleasant to him, he defends himself from exemplariness with ridicule, like those men who zealously guard their freedom, by dressing themselves up in irony in order to protect themselves from the captivating requests of a beautiful woman.

What can be said of choteo, in general terms, is that it denotes an inconsistency between internal appreciation and conduct. In certain frequent cases, that contradiction is explained, as we shall see, by a modest form of irony; but even then, the ridicule has an origin in that impatience that the criollo feels, on account of his temperament, toward any obstacle in the way of his free expansion, toward any not overly imperative kind of exemplariness.

Choteo, "Guataquería,"[18] Rebellion

It seems to me that this also helps to understand the use of
the word in the sense of denunciation. In schools, barracks,
and prisons, "*chota*" is what you call a companion who
snitches on others to authority. It denotes, without a doubt,
he who surrenders officiously, not very far from what is so in
style today under the infamous stigma of "guataquería." But
that is precisely why the word "chota" involves a reproach,
and if the one who informs does so to ingratiate himself
with the powerful, the name "chota" is given to him since
his betrayal reveals and, therefore, thwarts a hidden intent;
that is to say, it takes away the authority and prestige from
his secret. From the moment when the private becomes the
public domain, or the exclusive is popularized, it is deval-
ued, "choteado." We say the same about a show that everyone has already seen. Merchants declare that this happens
to goods when there are so many for sale that they cannot
charge whatever they please (exercising over the goods the
authority of a virtual monopoly), but rather have to strictly
abide by the law of supply and demand.

In all regards, choteo is, as we can see, an enemy to whatever proposes a limitation on individual growth. Something
else occurs when the limitation is imposed, rather than pro-
posed. Therefore, the spirit of independence that always
boils at the bottom of choteo has two ways of escaping: either outright rebellion or flattery. Both are ways to claim
greater agency than one has. Rebellion produced the Republic; flattery has spawned that thing that we now call "guataquería." But, as soon as that authority is weak, indirect or
unarmed, choteo emerges as a self-affirmation.

18 T.N. "Guataquería" refers to flattery with a strategy in mind.

Now we would not find anything of particular interest in the fact that its name came from "*choto*," "*cabrito*" (kid), because the word "*capricho*" (caprice) also comes from "*cabra*" (goat). And what the *choteador* or *chota* instinctively defends is his absolute freedom when it comes to whims and improvisation. Therefore, he jokingly abhors every principle of conduct and every disciplinary demand—absolute accuracy, punctuality, the conscientious, the ritual and the ceremonial, the methodical—in short, whatever serves to rigorously channel an individual's force or to link it—with unavoidable yet effective rigidity—to the mechanism of the collective force.

Based on the preceding argument, perhaps we can infer a tighter and more formal definition of choteo than the one that served us at the start. Choteo *is an urge for independence that appears in the form of mockery of any non-imperative form of authority.*

Choteo, Humor, Wit, Gracia

That said, is this choteo that we have been analyzing the one that is often considered a national characteristic?

There exists, as we know, an insistent tendency to presume that choteo is not a specific quality attributed to particular individuals, such as impulsivity, egoism, falsehood, and the like; instead it is something that all of us Cubans have, in greater or lesser degree, diluted within our criollo idiosyncrasy. Something like a peculiar tropical psyche with which we condemn or save ourselves.

Those who make this assumption will surely find that the interpretation of choteo I just set forth is too pejorative to be acceptable. Apart from those previous conclusions, some will raise other objections. They might have thought or might think that not all instances of choteo correspond to that definition—that our typical mockery is not always an indication of licentiousness or a systematic rebellion. Anyway, perhaps they have missed the pure sympathy in my analysis, that healthy and fun approval—born from something other than a simple tolerance toward one's weaknesses—that inspires instances of vernacular humor in us.

But, my friends, couldn't it be that those alleged nonconformists are thinking precisely about criollo humor, wit, or gracia, and not about choteo? Since this notion has been so confusing among us, the word has lent itself to every possible misunderstanding. Additionally, in ordinary language, there is a natural hyperbolism, a tendency to always designate things by their more extreme related manifestations, even though doing so does away with accuracy. Who hasn't at one point or another heard our newspaper vendors passionately dispute a sale, reproaching others for nothing less than "lust"? Of course, in reality, what they mean to say is vehemence, greed, passion—words that are not in their dictionary. In this way, choteo has been used, and quite frequently, to denote utmost jocularity with regard to facts, sayings, and laughable situations that are not at all choteo. Rather, they should be understood as part of criollo people's share in universal gracia.

But our choteo does not have anything to do with our gracia; or, to say it more precisely, choteo is, in any case, a special and systematic form of gracia.

There are those who suppose that choteo is a peculiar Cuban reaction against excessive seriousness. Although always elemental, that interpretation would be accurate if we understand "the excessively serious" as a reference to everything bearing authority. Such a notion is not uncommon among us. Our most frivolous youth usually considers the ceremonious man too serious, even though in reality he could be very jovial at the same time. Certain public writers who, in social settings, are the least solemn of people have a reputation for being "excessively serious" on account of the didactic or clarifying tone that they adopt in their journalistic work, as if teaching and clarifying were not part of the function of modern journalism.

It is certain, then, that choteo uses mockery to attack or dodge everything that is too serious, if by that, anything the choteador deems too authoritative or exemplary is understood. But to try and say that choteo only mocks unpleasant packaging or ridiculous gravity is inaccurate, since that explanation does not suffice for a series of phenomena that are precisely the most typical of choteo. For example, consider the following event that I was once able to witness. In the living room of a house there is a young lady singing at the piano. She sings a sentimental ballad, but nothing lachrymose or solemn. Moreover, she sings well, so well that some young people on the sidewalk listen to her in silence, entranced. When the woman stops, however, the young people move away from the window, and in a pompous voice, ruthlessly ridicule the same gift that just delighted them. In this situation where is the reaction against the excessively serious or grave? Aren't we really talking about a custom of mockery that systematically stands up against all that is prestigious even when it is pleasant?

Either choteo is that absolute and systematic attitude, or on the contrary, we have no basis on which to distinguish it as a modality apart from mockery. And if we agree that it is a systematic mockery, then there is nothing more opposed to humor.

"It is unquestionable," says Pío Baroja in *La caverna del humorismo,* "that where there is a level of seriousness, respectability, there is another level of laughter and mockery. The tragic, the epic, are lodged in the foreground; the comical in the background. The comedian jumps constantly from one to another and goes so far as to confuse the two, and that is why humor can be defined as the seriously comical, the transcendental trivial, the sad, philosophical, and cosmic laughter."[19] But choteo deliberately ignores that level of respectability about which Baroja speaks and, like a stubborn tenant, installs itself on the level of the comical. Nor does it ever perceive in this a reflection of the sublime that is, for Lipps, what illuminates the comedian from within. This

19 T.N. Pío Baroja, *La caverna del humorismo* (Madrid: Rafael Caro Raggio, 1919), 59. An English translation has not been published. Note that Pío Baroja refers to "la risa triste, filosófica y cósmica" while Mañach's publication incorrectly quotes the text as "la risa triste, filosófica y cómica."

is not to say, of course, that the choteador cannot sometimes be a comedian. However, that coincidence is not very frequent, because for the comedian, deep human feeling is essential, and for the choteador, selfishness, an urge for personal independence. Anyway, there is no need to identify instances of humor with those of choteo even though it may be the same individual who reveals them.

Choteo is neither our wit nor our gracia. There is always a mental acuteness in wit of which typical choteo, generally impressionistic and superficial mockery, does not tend to be capable. Wit is of such an intellectual nature that it always appears respectful of manifestations higher than itself. A clever man will always respond to another's attack with a greater show of spirit, like in that famous debate among English parliamentarians, described by Varona. If a man cannot overcome adverse wit, he will surrender like a gentleman. However, choteo is so minimally intellectual that, when faced with an ingenious feint, it responds with a new, infuriating mockery. It is not a genre of dialectics, but of assault. Here though one should recognize that choteo and wit are not necessarily incompatible. They are simply two different types that do not get along well.

Cuban gracia is, in fact, more closely linked to choteo. That gracia, as its very name indicates, is a natural gift, something alien from individuals' culture and from their mentality. In my opinion, comedic gracia consists of a certain disposition and clarity of mind, the kind that everything bounces elastically off, without penetrating, without leaving any trace. This form of optimism constantly seeks to justify itself, smoothing over the edges of reality. Because of this, gracia is predominantly feminine and not bitter in the least. It does not aspire to challenge but rather to avoid. Because its festive longing is only for happiness, for vital comfort, it insists on seeing the world without dangers, without thorns, or cliffs.

That said, one can clearly deduce that an exaggeration of the spirit of gracia can lead to the negation of all values. The desire to smooth things over is likely to become an obsession with flattening all that is bumpy. And beginning by coveting the vital comfort of happiness, it is possible to go so far as to demand that vital luxury, which is absolute independence from all authority. As a result of diverse factors that we shall soon see, a light and healthy mockery born from gracia is somehow corrupted by systematization so much that it turns into choteo.

But this is not fatal. To suppose that the same corruption operates in all Cubans is, of course, an absurd exaggeration. That very gracia is not the privilege of the entire tropical species. Solemn Cubans, serious Cubans, who are incapable of choteo, are more abundant than one would think, just as there is many an Andalusian bereft of humor. What can and should be established is that within the Cuban idiosyncrasy there are peculiar characteristics. At times, they are caused by, and, at others, they are attributed to the weather or the social circumstances in which we have been developing, and they tend to facilitate that perversion of mockery we call choteo.

Levity and Independence

Of these traits, the one most frequently emphasized, is criollo levity.

Ramiro Guerra, in a praise-worthy chapter of his *Historia de Cuba* (*History of Cuba*), declares that the Cuban "is apparently only stubborn in his levity," and he seems to substantiate that claim when he adds that "the main weakness of his character lies in that lack of aptitude to accept an attitude and to wholly devote himself to it, infusing it with all the vigor and strength from his soul."[20] In this sense, then, levity is inconsistency. But, to what psychological constitution is he responding?

Even within the linguistic connotations of the word, levity is a lack of gravity; and what we mean metaphorically by this is a lack of deliberation, of an aptitude to weigh things exactly. From what does it result, if not a lack of adequate attention? Sustained attention is what invites reflection, a return to the first aspect of what has been judged, measuring its importance and its scope exactly.

This lack of sufficient attention—which, as we saw, is one of the conditions of disrespect—originates from excessive impressionability, which the Cuban shares with all tropical peoples. For the same reason that our senses are constantly kept alert under the whip of the relentless sun, criollo intelligence is instantly impressionable, but what happens to it is what happens to instantaneous photographs: the image is only clear at first and the impression does not last long. In other words, our average mentality lacks a sense of the third dimension—the dimension of depth. We see things more as

20 T.N. Ramiro Guerra, *Historia de Cuba* (Havana: El Siglo XX, 1921), 67.

a contoured view than in relief. The deepest of implications, the most distant of reaches, almost always escape us. Hence, we treat life a little like a stage. We don't recognize anything as sufficiently real to take it very seriously, nor as important enough to give in to it entirely.

A Spanish serviceman from the last century, General Concha, who had the opportunity to observe us up close, declared that our cheerfulness boiled down to "a little tiple guitar music, a little cock fighting, and a little game of cards." Like every caricature, the phrase has elements of truth, even though it may be very subjective. The diminutives we use already allude to that tendency of ours to "baby" words, a tendency that is not due as much to an emotional exuberance as it is to another feature that we shall see: that of familiarity, not placing too much importance on anything, putting everything on the level of the most intimate. But the phrase is also significant because it limits our ambition (and implicitly our capacity for passion) to fun and games.

Our love of gambling, which we are the first to recognize as something that defines us, would merit a study apart. Nothing more complex than the player's emotion. In it, there's a curious mixture of audacity and fear, vehemence and caution, of generosity and greed. But the fact that interests us now is that this love of gambling is usually characteristic of all impressionable nations. When the certainty and tranquility of the future are subordinated to the emotion of a given moment, it is because sufficient foresight, or rather, the capacity to evaluate in the abstract, is lacking.

In that psychological trait, the foundations of one of our most beautiful qualities—disinterest—can be seen. What exactly is the interested being, but one who evaluates too much in perspective, one who practices a kind of opportunism?

Even when it comes to explaining the economic fact of bank interest, the interested being resorts to the phenomenon of perspective: as his possession moves away, money gets tighter like train rails that narrow in the distance. Interest is the compensation for that narrowing. The Cuban is not interested, because he lacks the habit or the mental optics for projecting things into the future. His retina, like that of certain insects, does not focus equally on the first and last terms. For him, the superficial and profound are placed on the same level of appreciation, and therefore, of assessment. Present satisfaction is what matters. Hence a peculiar mix of virtues and defects: our generosity, our hedonism; however naive in our malice and docile in our indiscipline; susceptible to apparent flattery and censorship; our indifference toward undertakings of importance, our utilitarian zeal despite our generosity, and finally, our choteo.

The other cardinal feature of our character is independence. Not independence of a wild and savage sort, but rather one that is peaceful and evasive. Ganivet said that the Spaniards' ideal can be expressed with one traditional phrase: "*hacer su real gana.*"[21] Perhaps we have inherited that spirit from Spaniards, but within us, it takes on a less unruly and active form. The Cuban is generally contented as long as he is not bothered. He couldn't care less about freedom in the abstract, as long as it does not end up affecting his agency. He remains insensitive and even acquiescent to the arrogations and the excessive demands of authority as long as he doesn't feel the injury at his core. We are, as Ortega y Gasset already observed in Spaniards, more sensitive to violations of private jurisdiction than those of public,

---

21 T.N. To do whatever you damn please.

and we do not opt to protest unless an excess of power limits personal independence.

This independence is defended against all relationships that impose a limit, a restraint. Hence the Cuban instinctively tends to abolish every hierarchy and to situate all things and values on the same level of familiarity. In this way, the oft-mentioned criollo familiarity is born, that is, perhaps, the most visible and pronounced trait of our character.

When we come to Cuba from abroad—especially if we come from a country of heavier moods, the United States, or even France, for example—from the very moment of stepping onto the docks, we are surprised by a certain atmosphere of looseness and of stentorian camaraderie that seems to be the social climate of Cuba, corresponding to its physical warmth and brightness. Right there, on the threshold of the Island, the baggage or hotel attendant will approach us without that servile helpfulness that his colleagues from other latitudes have. He'll call us "buddy" and treat us as though he had always been reserving the most effusive camaraderie for us. A few more hours of immersion in the tropical environment convince us that we have come to a land totally devoid of gravity, etiquette, and distance. Nowhere among Cubans do we see that circumspection, that restraint, that selfish absorption in their own business that turns the performance of Nordic countries, and European countries in general, into "a symphony in gray major." Everything in Cuba has the laughter of its light, the lightness of its clothes, the frankness of its homes open to passing curiosity. No sign of austerity or hierarchy impresses us. On the contrary, a squandering of energy, of wealth, of trust, can be observed everywhere. People talk loudly, they get drunk on the overflow from the cups, the alcohol-drenched wood in the cantinas. The automobile has lost the methodical seriousness of the taximeter and has instead become a vehicle in which the chauffeur tells us the most obsequious secrets from the driver's seat. We are in the perfect republic. Everything is everyone's. And as the kindled and vibrant light seems to annul distance and chiaroscuro, a spiritual luminosity that radiates from everyone's faces annuls social distance and levels all hierarchical projections.

No one can be surprised by the fact that in such an environment there is a tendency toward the systematic annulment of due respect, which is choteo. The Cuban's independent spirit leads him to abolish authority, even in social matters. The informal second person form of address prevails and the most important people respond to their first names, if not to diminutives thereof, or to affectionate nicknames. But I already said that more than affection, what exists is egalitarianism, familiarity, or, to say it using a word with very similar connotations: "parejería"[22]: And be careful of us all being on par with one another.

Rather, the relationship that this egalitarian instinct has with choteo is no less evident than the one that our Cuban levity has with it. We already saw that choteo was either produced by a lack of attention or an inadequate sense of authority. Where we are all esteemed and treated as equals, there is no authority. An English proverb warns that famil-

22 Here I'm restoring what appears to be the primary meaning of this word that is so much ours. In effect, it has come to assume, by derivation, that of "a person who puts on airs, who considers himself superior," an attitude that is contrary to egalitarianism. Nevertheless, that meaning comes from the same idea of presumption that was associated with the word when primarily it was employed, as is well-known, to designate individuals of color who conducted themselves as white, who "caught up with/made themselves equal to" him.

iarity breeds contempt. And certainly, while criollo familiarity has plenty of interesting characteristics, expressions of respect and true humor are not among them. Familiarity only fosters mockery. Pío Baroja has aptly remarked upon the possibilities of humor increasing "the more proficient the style, the rhetoric, and the seriousness there is on one level of life.... In Naples, Seville, or Valencia," he adds, "there has been no sense of humor, in comparison with the humor of London and that's because English life is, of all European lives, the most solid, the most traditional and the most solemn."[23] In a deep sense, this is also what our Varona pointed out, when he wrote that "the English people's humor is one of the manifestations of their being conscious of their strength,"[24] that is to say, in taking themselves seriously. The small nation's awareness that, on account of its weakness, it is not respected, makes everyone within it respect each other less, dissolving those contrasts that invite humor.

These two spiritual dispositions of ours—levity and independence—have been, thus, the breeding ground for choteo. But they naturally produce nothing more than a benign choteo: so to speak, a certain ironic and skeptical jocularity that could be the substratum of the Cuban gracia, like it is of the Andalusian gracia. The experts on Andalusia assure us that a similar environment and attitude can be observed there; and we cannot forget—although we should not attribute disproportionate importance to this fact, as sometimes happens—that a good number of our Spanish ances-

<hr>

23 T.N. Pío Baroja, 113.
24 T.N. Enrique José Varona, *Desde mi belvedere* (1907) (Caracas, Ayacucho, 2010), 330.

tors were Andalusian. Reading Quinteros' comedies,[25] we note that their gracia has many similarities with the benign criollo choteo. So far, it is not a gracia of universal meaning, but rather one conditioned by the environment in which it is produced. Hence, the Quinterian comedies are difficult to translate; their comicalness, faintly sprinkled with wit, would not move a Scotsman or a German to laughter. Furthermore, like in Cuba, we are dealing with a certain *san façon*, a perennial lack of inhibition, an independent and hedonistic sense of life, resistant toward all excessive social restraint.

But this Andalusian humor also, like ours, carries in itself the seeds of a fermentation that often turns it into something toxic and overflowing. In the same way that the exaggeration of Cuban gracia produces choteo in its most pernicious form, the exaggeration of Andalusian gracia is what they call "*pitorreo*," a regional phenomenon that is almost identical to ours, about which Américo Castro recently provided me with intelligent and harsh commentary. The individualism that informs the Spanish conception of life, combined with a certain fatalistic sensualism of African origin, all heated up by a climate that is not very different from ours, establishes that similarity between the Andalusian and the Cuban.

25 T.N. Mañach refers to the brothers Serafín and Joaquín Álvarez Quintero, born in Seville, in 1871 and 1873 respectively, and writers primarily of comedies.

Choteo and Improvisation

It is clear that peculiar external factors have intervened in the formation of our choteo.[26]

Unequivocally choteo has most benefited from our rapid and prosperous collective evolution.

There is a relationship of reciprocal influence between the character and the experience of a people. If national idiosyncrasy models history its own way, I also believe that history itself leaves its mark on character. This is perhaps due to a fact that to me is evident: national character is not as fixed as it is assumed. Political events of transcendental importance, the ebbs and flows of economic prosperity, the diversity of customs—determined in large part by differences in role models and norms of conduct—cause forms of behavior to appear and stand out from the complex depths of a people's idiosyncrasy. These forms of behavior respond

---

26　The contact with the African psychology, to which I just alluded, could be one of them. In part on account of sloth, in part, on account of social and intellectual pusillanimity, that influence still has not been studied among us with the care and the rigor that must be put into it, if we want to become aware of our national complex. I do not pretend to insinuate here that the black is an agent of choteo. On the contrary, he contributes to our relational life more solemnity, seriousness, and respect than could be imagined. Perhaps Paul Morand sins for superficiality, in his recent *Magpie Noir*, when he asks himself, "Ignore-t-il que Dieu a fait don aux nègres de son plus précieux trésor: la joie?" Even so, it doesn't seem to me to be improbable that the man of color, with his wealth of never-revealed vitality, on account of his impressionable and sensual nature and his lack of that pessimism that accompanies secular jobs in our civilization, has accentuated certain criollo traits that, in the white man, when joined with other psychic factors, turn out to be propitious to choteo.

to diverse external situations, and consequently they vary immensely.[27]

If in biology, the function creates the organ, in psychology, the appropriate or obligatory attitude often creates what we call the character trait. In this way, it is logical that during the liberation period the Cuban was prone to irony or taciturnity, the same way he is now to frankness and mockery. Back then, the Spanish vigilance of attitudes required a cautious restraint; the spectacle of the homeland doing everything it could for its own dignity and the fatigue and deprivations that led to attaining the homeland could not but occasion our concealing joy, since this is always an indication of vital comfort.

Conversely, once the Republic came about, economic restoration was so rapid and so rich that an aventurine atmosphere was created. Ownership and being in charge were relatively accessible privileges. We saw, settling into power and exercising authority, those men who had earned that right in the countryside, alongside others whom we had addressed informally in the rumor mills and salons. Improvisation had to rule for a long time in all areas of Cuban life; and just as institutions and representatives were created overnight to take charge, for better or worse, of public service; in other areas—in teaching, in the professional realm and in arts and literature, organs and agents were also im-

27 This is so much the case that I'm adding this note in 1955. These days, one can affirm, if not the disappearance in Cuba of choteo since those critical years that came a little after I wrote this essay, at least, its attenuation. The revolutionary process that was so tense, so anguished and so bloody, at times, of the 30s and 40s came to dramatize the Cuban, sometimes leading him to tragic excesses. Today, choteo is no longer the nearly ubiquitous phenomenon that it was in the past. Now the raspberry is hardly heard. History goes about modifying our character bit by bit.

provised and hardly ideal. It would not be difficult, I think, to pinpoint the influence of the recent garrulous and provincial journalism that we've had to endure on the criollo character. Or for that matter, the intellectual social climber who become a teacher, the professional who has acquired mythical prestige, the politician with an undisclosed background, the magazine that has wanted to be comical, but is merely scandalous, or the farce that, under the guise of *criollismo*, has hidden only crass pornography and a schematic plebeianism. This whole enlisted troop, all these impersonations—sometimes through direct indoctrination of false criteria and spurious tastes, others through ineptitude when it comes to defending what is truly valuable—corrupted us into superficiality, skepticism, or buffoonery, prompting the breakdown of respect, an extremely delicate attitude, which therefore counters the unruly appetite of instinct.

The social environment, then, with these inevitable mystifications and improvisations, has contributed so powerfully to fostering the anti-hierarchical spirit of our mockery, which could almost be said to have engendered choteo. More than an innate tendency within our character, this is the result of a particular collective experience. It's born out of an environment rather than an idiosyncrasy. I have had the opportunity to confirm this in my frequent encounters with Cuban students abroad. In the United States and in France I have noticed that they behave in the most circumspect manner and with joviality only in good taste, while then here in Cuba, I have seen these young compatriots possessed by the devilish choteo. It is the spectacle of distorted authority that exacerbates the natural critical spirit of Cuban gracia.

Effects of Choteo

Along with the most dire effects within the moral and cultural order, choteo has exercised, in certain cases, a healthy critical function. Since it consistently mocks all that is official, sometimes it has to get right.

Not all authorities are just or desirable, and that's why mockery was always a resource for the oppressed—whatever the nature of the oppression. Chronic mockery has been one of the Cuban's greatest ailments, as much as it has been one of his greatest defenses. It has served him in absorbing the shocks of adversity: as a spring to resist political pressures that are too burdensome and as an escape from all kinds of restlessness. In other words, it has been a very effective source of relief for us. Since what it sets out to maneuver is to diminish the importance of things, that is to say, to prevent them from affecting us too much, choteo emerges in any situation in which the criollo spirit sees itself as embittered by a false or hardly flexible authority.

When this authority, whatever its jurisdiction, is genuine and has imperial reason, choteo cannot be justified except as an infantile vice of a nation that hasn't yet had time to mature, and above all to mature naturally, without the assistance of others. But when, as so often it happens, it is a matter of a hollow or improvised authority, or for whatever excessive reason, from an authority *whose shape does not correspond to its substance*, which claims more than it is really worth, then choteo is a formidable informer, and it is helped a lot by its very lack of great satirical pretensions, its very simplicity.

The emergency weapon in such cases tends to be the raspberry. In the entire repertoire of derogatory emissions and gestures that we have at our disposal, the raspberry is the most humiliating one, and perhaps also the one most loaded with abject allusions. There is nothing so grave, as imperturbable as it may be, that the raspberry's strident dash of disdain can't permeate, at least momentarily. Its effectiveness is in its very lack of violence, in the belittling achieved by its very diminutive tone. Any other gesture of mockery or disdain—to stick out one's tongue, to refuse a handshake, to spit at another—involves a direct attack that strengthens insulted dignity. Instead the raspberry, no matter how oblique and distant, seems to disarm and even momentarily dissolve the dignity at which it is directed. It is a tiny dart that always lands on the target—at the center of gravity— waving the banner of ridicule. Of course, it turns out to be too crude, and often too frivolous and irresponsible to constitute more than a momentary sanction: too unworthy itself to undermine the excess of dignity that we call excessive prosopopeia.

But there is no doubt that certain sanctions of the minor kind are sometimes healthy. For example: nobodies en masse come to Cuba, anxious to regain prestige worn out in their homeland. To ours, they arrive as if to conquer, inflated with a sense of self-importance. The jesting in our country deflates them in time. And the native also has to think three times before becoming conceited. In his domestic intimacy, the tropical narcissist can gaze at his image without anyone infringing; but as soon as he tries to parade it around and to make a public authority out of an intimate illusion, choteo gets in the way and takes the wind out of his sails.

True choteo—that is, the systematic kind—collaborates with Cuban gracia, which functions as its substratum, on that sanction. This may not be systematic, but it is very demanding. The Cuban's lack of meaningful insight, of a sense of depth and distance, often deprives him of appreciating at first glance (which is usually the only thing he cultivates) the significance or implications of any fact. Hence all values have to become powerfully marked, solidly and categorically, for the average Cuban to assess them. But then no one respects them anymore, even if they are not complied with or put into practice. If mediocrity is so tolerated in Cuba, it is because intolerance presumes an authority, a repulsive thing in itself. The Cuban rejects it in the same way he rejects all superstition, all dogma, or bigotry. He'd be a great propagandist of free inquiry, if he weren't so impressionable as to cultivate that inquiry as an attitude. But to get him to truly accept mediocrity, it is essential to touch what triggers his feelings.

And nevertheless, as in almost all peoples of our lineage, in the Cuban those emotional triggers are extremely tense and reactive. No one gets excited with more ease or with more puerility than Cubans. Politicians, who constantly make use of an oratory device which they call "getting to the fiber of the people" know that hyperesthesia well, that soft and exposed spot that is always embodied in the criollo. Typical Cuban songs denounce it with notorious eloquence. It has even been said that, "deep down," we are a people of intense melancholy. How do you reconcile that with choteo, which is habitual mockery and merriness?

Here, choteo also acts as a spiritual decongestant, rebelling against the authority of sentiment. The Cuban is such a "show-off," so protective of his independence that he does not want to appear trapped by his own emotion. Many times, at the theater, at the movies, we note that some spectator nearby laughs or says something funny in the most pathetic moment of the performance. We usually consider him a brute. Sometimes he is, but other times, he is a poor devil with a lump in his throat. Choteo then becomes an act of shame, a layer of jocularity that we take upon ourselves to hide our inner sadness, for fear of appearing tender or spiritual.

Francisco Figueras relates, in a very valuable and quite forgotten book, like all our good books, a patriotic anecdote that he deems expressive of the "Voltarianism" of our character, but without emphasizing that element of modesty that informs Cuban irony: "G. del C., one of the medical students condemned to prison in 1871, wore a splendid blonde beard that made him look like a young lord. As shots rang out, putting an end to his classmates' lives, G. del. C, who had just suffered tonsure, donned the suit and clinched the regulatory chain of prison, entered the dungeon where his companions awaited their turn in the gloomy toilette—'Ecce homo,' he said to them."[28] No doubt, everyone laughed along with the phrase, but it's likely that they were also swallowing their tears.

Such modest irony is, perhaps, the only kind that the Cuban practices skillfully. All irony is more or less a form of simulation, of duplicity, since it consists of saying the opposite of what is felt or thought. But the Cuban is so sincere—sincere even when lying, something he does without scruples—that every ironic form of contestation repulses him. He prefers choteo that is forthright ridicule, openly displayed, generally nothing that is pointed like a dart, but more like the fine dust of ground-up ribbing that is tossed

28 Quoted in *Cuba y su evolución colonial*, Havana, 1907.

in the victim's face.[29] Choteo disturbs the victim not with its forcefulness, but rather with its suffocating environment of allusions and misunderstandings that form around the victim. Sometimes, its method is that of the diatribe; it limits itself to going about undressing, stripping its victim, piece by piece, of all the clothes in which vanity or gravity is hidden. At other times, as in the current case of a certain politician that choteo insists on presenting as a quaint case of illiteracy, our mockery is brutal. Toward anything more or less weak, mockery twists it, enlarges it, and in the manner of caricature, eventually turns Narcissus into a monster.

As we can see, all these effects of the average choteo, of the kind that is widespread and casual, bordering on pure gracia, are at least innocent. When choteo is glaringly pernicious is when it becomes absolute and habitual, meaning, when it is not a sporadic reaction, but rather a habit, an attitude taken toward life. This kind of choteo, par excellence, turns out to be a perversion of Cuban humor, nothing other than salt in the land of sugar. I don't believe that this vice or quality is absolutely peculiar to us. There are other nations that have a gracia that is similar to ours and in which that gracia suffers equivalent corruption. But the fact is our word "choteo" is particular and with it, we indiscriminately designate our vice and our jocular virtue.

When choteo has been criticized, identifying its alarming moral and social state, systematic choteo and not Cuban gracia has been the focus. And, in effect, that systematic choteo is responsible for a large part of the slow speed with which we have progressed toward achieving a certain so-

29 T.N. I have adopted from Marta Hernández Salván's translation of this passage in *Minima Cuba: Heretic Poetics and Power in Post-Soviet Cuba* (Albany: Suny, 2015), 189.

cial and cultural decorum. Due to a blindly individualistic nature, the choteador is incapable of all tasks in which method, discipline, long and sustained effort, and constant reflection are requisites. Nevertheless, at worst, he is like a proverbial dog in the manger. The choteador has been the obstacle, the guzzler of enthusiasm par excellence, getting nourishment from it. Wherever a glimmer of hope is perceived, a determination to seek a better life, the guzzler, the choteador's mockery, is immediately applied.

I will mention an example. Recall the ridicule that used to take place in our university of those students who were eager to learn. We used to call them nerds, chase them as if they were traitors to a juvenile cause that had as its principle the sacred right of idleness. Of course, a lot of that was mere juvenile frivolity, but that mockery also extended to other more responsible and mature sectors in society. It even contaminated public opinion. If, throughout the world, the intellectual takes in a greater or lesser degree of indifference, here he usually inhales the asphyxiating gases of choteo. And not out of a simple primitive hatred toward culture, but rather because culture, as the superb Argentine essayist, Arturo Cancela, reminds us, entails a servitude, a discipline.[30] The greater the rigor the intellectual puts into his work, the more he has been ridiculed among us.

On account of that same servitude to the ideal, the politician who took on the task of governing the people or legislating for them seriously—"romantically," as they used to say—was made fun of. In this way, choteo enthroned shamelessness, the "a little more, a little less attitude," a form of social climbing in all realms of activity. And it came

30 Arturo Cancela, *Palabras socráticas de Arturo Cancela* (Buenos Aires, M. Gleizer Publisher, 1928).

to undermine the sense of authority so deeply, that for quite some time, it made all critique that was not part of its own lineage, that is to say, streaked with irresponsible mockery, impossible or unpleasant.

To this last influence, we singularly owe that confusion and intellectual informality that we observe, and still suffer from, in our midst. It is still difficult to gain authority in Cuba; it is difficult, at the very least, to make it worthwhile. Although the nucleus of public opinion is always more or less intensely sensitive to merit, that vigilant solidarity, that noble collective willingness to defend genuine courage, which in other countries constitutes the principal guarantee of any elevated and honest situation, still hasn't formed among us. Likewise, our public opinion, even when it is most convinced of a value's authenticity, lacks that coherency between conviction and conduct that Ramiro Guerra discovered in the Cuban individual. It is always possible for any mere dabbler to think he has the right to discuss the impressions of the most authoritative specialist, and for the talented and dedicated to find themselves at the mercy of the first fool who refutes them, sometimes with a pen in hand.

I would still go on in detail about the pernicious influences that can be attributed to choteo in the moral and social order, if I hadn't already exhausted your generous attention too much. On the other hand, my goal has been less to consider the extremely well-known effects of that phenomenon than to explore its nature. Having analyzed this nature, the consequences are mostly evident. In general terms, one can say that choteo has tended to instill in our people the fear of all noble forms of distinction—the fear of being "too" intellectual, too spiritual, too courteous, and even too sensible or elegant. Who doesn't recall, in effect, a time when it became impossible to go out on the streets of Havana—not in an admittedly ridiculous cloak and top hat anymore, but in a mere overcoat on severe winter days?

Choteo's Transience

But, fortunately, we are speaking about an era that is almost entirely behind us. While choteo has been the result of an atmosphere, it has also been of a certain period that is already nearing its end—the period we could call one of improvisation in our national life. The qualities of our character that constitute the psychological elements utilized by choteo are inherent, and although not irrevocably fixed, indeed are very slow to modify. No matter how much blood is diluted and customs altered, our climate will always be there to ensure we are somewhat light, impressionable, jocular, and melancholic at the same time, and those will be the foundations of our native humor. What has to be prevented is the degeneration of gracia into choteo, and I think that can only go about being achieved on its own each day with the gradual advent of our maturity, with the gradual alteration of our social climate. As we become more numerous, richer, and more refined, as we eliminate our primitive village mentality from our young nation, we can increase our sense of hierarchy and diminish, as a result, the living conditions that create choteo.

Nevertheless, it would not hurt to make every effort to activate this evolution, saturating our environment with those subtle essences of respect that are the antidote to unmeasured mockery. Fundamentally, this is an enterprise of education. Aptitude for respect is, ultimately, aptitude for *evaluating* and, therefore, it depends on the degree of culture an individual possesses—on the kind of culture that does not consist so much of a broad body of knowledge as of a fruitful discipline of the spirit, on a deep longing for rapport with "all that, in nature and history, is essential in the world."

We shall always remember Chesterton's gleaming astonishment. One day, when faced with respectful peasants of Castile, he exclaimed, "How cultured are these illiterate folks!"[31] In Cuba up until now, we have been exceptionally dedicated to making literate men, erudite men, but not to making cultured men. Our education has not only been flawed in that it has failed to correct certain immoral psychic inclinations in certain individuals that, like envy and its byproduct, resentment, incubate systematic choteo; in addition, it has neglected to offer our youth norms, criteria, perspectives, and incentives for perfection. In our homes, there has been a general lack of a true normative spirit. At most, a disciplinary mood has prevailed, but in a coercive and dogmatic way, without instilling in children habits of reflection that would enable them to evaluate on their own. At school and at the university, the excessive positivism of an education with very limited individual specification, which is more attuned to getting ahead than to discovering cultural landscapes, has also deprived our youth of exercising their own sense of critique, of disciplining their curiosities, and infusing their cheerfulness with authentic enthusiasm.

31 T.N. Fernando de los Ríos reports this conversation in the book, *La filosofía política de Platón* (The Political Philosophy of Plato, 1907), published in his *Obras completas* (Madrid: Caja de Madrid, 1997), 55. De los Ríos delineates a list of Chesterton's observations that include how the country folk ate, held their knives, cut cheese, onions, and bread. He also refers to these activities as the "aesthetic prodigy of refinement." The word that de los Ríos reports as having been used as "cultos" or "cultured," seems imprecise in this instance, however, it is compatible with what Mañach goes on to discuss.

Cheerfulness and Audacity

Genuine enthusiasm, I mean.

The purpose of this lecture would have been greatly missed if it left the impression that, in condemning systematic choteo, I have also wanted to belittle or look down upon those manifestations of jovial wit that are the salt of life, or that clean and healthy cheerfulness whose cultivation is precisely the slogan of our time. That very mockery is sometimes just and necessary. Gracián said, "Some things are to be taken laughing, and the very same sometimes that others take in good earnest,"[32] but "pleasantry and jesting being only the seasoning of conversation...ought to be regulated and proportioned as that is in our Sauces," and the worst thing of all is ending up "hired [just] to divert Company and make them laugh."[33]

Cheerfulness is even more appealing, because when it is authentic, it reveals a youthfulness on the inside, a richness of vitality that multiplies our enthusiasm for all tasks of any endeavor. If, for some reason, the art of our time sustains a spirited reaction against the romanticism of our elders, it is precisely because melancholic and lachrymose romanticism lacked that energetic cheerfulness of a hooray, which stirs up, like a conquest or an aspiration, even the most dramatic art of the moment.

Finally, in invoking the need for more and greater respect, I have not wanted to clip the wings of the native spirit of independence that conquered our public liberties and that is

32 T.N. Baltasar Gracián, *The Courtiers Manual Oracle or the Art of Prudence* (1601-1658) (London: Miles Flesher for Abel Swalle, 1685), 78.
33 T.N. Baltasar Gracián, *The Compleat Gentleman*, trans. T. Saldkeld (London: P. Lord, 1760), 50-53.

the deepest guarantee of their preservation. On the contrary, I believe that in many realms of our endeavors we still lack fearlessness and audacity. But just as cheerfulness (for it to be fruitful, to really illuminate our lives) must have true motives for satisfaction—diaphanous inner focal points of love and esteem—so too, audacity is only valid and decent when it is cultivated with responsibility and discipline.

We are experiencing a dawning of maturity in which, despite certain transitory ambiguities in the political realm, firm, clear outlines of the spirit are already present. Our critical faculty will increase in Cuba everywhere with the advent of our youth facing a greater collective experience. Choteo, like mental licentiousness, is on the defensive. The time has come to be critically cheerful, fastidiously audacious, and consciously disrespectful.

Jorge Mañach (1898-1961) is one of the most important Cuban thinkers of the 20th century. His activity as a philosopher, scholar, journalist, historian, and politician is an index of Cuba's dramas and conflicts at that time. Mañach, author of *Martí, El apóstol*, is largely responsible for not only construing the 20th century image of one of the nation's founders, but also for dissecting the conflicted relationship between Cuba and the United States, in the polemical Manifesto of the extremist political group ABC. His diverse list of writings include the foreword to a clandestine edition of Fidel Castro's famous 1953 speech, *"History Will Absolve Me."* He also belonged to the Cuban Association of the Congress for Cultural Freedom whose aim was to destroy anti-totalitarian thought worldwide.

Jacqueline Loss is a professor of Latin American Literary and Cultural Studies at the University of Connecticut. She is the author of *Dreaming in Russian: The Cuban Soviet Imaginary* (2013) and *Cosmopolitanisms and Latin America: Against the Destiny of Place* (2005) and co-editor of *Caviar with Rum: Cuba-USSR and the Post-Soviet Experience* (with José Manuel Prieto, 2012) and *New Short Fiction from Cuba* (with Esther Whitfield, 2007). Her essays and translations have appeared in *Nepantla, Chasqui, Latino and Latina Writers, La Habana Elegante, New Centennial Review, Bomb, La Gaceta, Kamchatka, Words Without Borders, The Brooklyn Rail,* among other publications. The Spanish translation of *Dreaming in Russian: The Cuban Soviet Imaginary* is forthcoming in Almenara Press.